BUSINESS START-UP PRACTICE

DANA SHILLING

Prentice-Hall, Inc.
Englewood Cliffs, New Jersey

Prentice-Hall International, Inc., *London*
Prentice-Hall of Australia, Pty. Ltd., *Sydney*
Prentice-Hall Canada, Inc., *Toronto*
Prentice-Hall of India Private Ltd., *New Delhi*
Prentice-Hall of Japan, Inc., *Tokyo*
Prentice-Hall of Southeast Asia Pte. Ltd., *Singapore*
Editora Prentice-Hall do Brasil Ltda., *Rio de Janeiro*
Prentice-Hall Hispanoamericana, S.A., *Mexico*

© 1987 *by*
PRENTICE-HALL, INC.
Englewood Cliffs, N.J.

This publication is designed to provide accurate and
authoritative information in regard to the subject
matter covered. It is sold with the understanding
that the publisher is not engaged in rendering legal,
accounting, or other professional service. If legal
advice or other expert assistance is required, the
services of a competent professional person should
be sought.
*...From the Declaration of Principles jointly adopted by a
Committee of the American Bar Association and a Committee
of Publishers and Associations.*

Library of Congress Cataloging-in-Publication Data

Shilling, Dana.
  Business start-up practice.

  Includes indexes.
  1. Business enterprises—United States.
I. Title.
KF1355.S53 1986   346.73'065   86-25602
                        347.30665

ISBN 0-13-107749-X

ABOUT THE AUTHOR: Dana Shilling is a graduate of the Harvard Law School and is a member of the
New York bar who devotes herself to legal writing, editing, and language simplification. She is the author
of five law-related books for the lay audience, and has worked on several legal looseleaf services, including
CCH's *Business Strategies.* She is the series editor for the *Prentice-Hall Law Practice Portfolios* series.

Printed in the United States of America

What This Portfolio Can Do for You

It is said that every lieutenant in Napoleon's army carried the baton of a field marshal in his knapsack. Similarly, sometimes it seems that every red-blooded American yearns to open a chocolate-chip cooky store, a software house, a restaurant, or a manufacturing company to produce some invention of one degree of "crackpottedness" or another.

To continue the military metaphor, the life expectancy of many of these new businesses is as brief as that of a First World War soldier facing trench warfare. Some of this fragility is caused by adverse economic conditions, undercapitalization, or poor business judgment on the part of the entrepreneur. There's not much you, the lawyer, can do about any of those. However, many businesses suffer or die because the business owner, unfamiliar with legal rules, violated a law or regulation, or engaged in conduct that enmeshed both the owner and fledgling company in litigation.

The prudent person considering a business start-up *should* get legal advice before taking any further steps. The lawyer must, in turn, make sure that the entrepreneur complies with all the necessary formalities. For example, some of the items that you may have to handle are as follows: If the business will not be incorporated but will use an artificial name, then an artificial name or "DBA" (Doing Business As) certificate must be filed. If the business *will* be incorporated, certain formalities of charter, bylaws, and formal meetings will be required. Franchise taxes will have to be paid. If the business has employees, procedures must be instituted for withholding taxes, and for paying such employer-paid taxes as FUTA and the employer component of FICA. These taxes must be paid on prescribed schedules; failure to do so will almost certainly lead to the closing of the business. Many businesses require licenses; it may also be necessary to obtain a zoning variance. Certain products are subject to federal or state licensing requirements. The client has every right to expect the lawyer who is handling the business start-up to be aware of these requirements, to make sure that all the necessary papers are filed, and that all consents are obtained.

The lawyer and client may also have a different relationship, one in which the lawyer acts as a counselor and planner as well as a technician. In such cases, the attorney can educate the client and make sure that legal formalities are satisfied. For example, a client may want to incorporate because he or she has overestimated its advantages but has underestimated the problems of doing so; or the client may have heard somewhere that a Delaware incorporation is advantageous for businesses that are not in fact located in Delaware; or the client may want to operate as a partnership on a "handshake" basis, unaware that this frequently leads partners to a "clenched-fist" basis within a short time.

Entrepreneurs who lack effective legal advice at every step of the way may find themselves violating the Blue Sky Laws or federal securities laws, or may deprive themselves of Subchapter S or other election when these mechanisms would be advantageous. In addition, unsophisticated clients may take out bank loans, buy equipment subject to a security agreement, and lease equipment without realizing that the security provisions of the three are contradictory. Or, the business itself may become a creditor, but may fail to protect itself by making appropriate UCC filings.

A business start-up practice involves reams of paper. Some of the papers are routine: there's not much to a Certificate of Incorporation beyond making sure that it's completed properly, submitted, and returned on time. Other business documents, however, offer rich possibilities for creativity and for preventing business problems through intelligent action. For example, the Articles of Incorporation and bylaws can be drafted to minimize the possibility of conflict between majority and minority shareholders. Perhaps there can be cumulative voting for directors (if, indeed, the state does not require cumulative voting); maybe the minority shareholders can combine to form a voting agreement or voting trust. In appropriate cases, the stockholders may agree to compulsory arbitration in case of corporate dissension.

There's no requirement that a partnership must have a charter or bylaws, of course; but the wise attorney can prevent endless difficulties later on by making sure that the partners agree to the following: a sound, well-drafted partnership agreement that specifies their mutual rights and duties; how much time each will spend on partnership business; the amount of capital and services each will contribute, and the accounting and tax status of such considerations; what the partners are entitled to receive as salary, guaranteed payments, and profit shares; how new partners may be added, or partners removed; and other crucial issues of both practical and tax import.

Although theoretically a corporation can have perpetual duration, in the real world corporate businesses seldom last for more than a generation. Either they perish in the first few years because of economic or management factors, or they are unable to survive the transition from the first generation of ownership and management to a second generation. Another service the attorney can provide is to counsel the client about the need for a buy-sell agreement. In either a partnership or corporate situation, the buy-sell agreement serves a variety of purposes. It makes sure that there will be a smooth transition when the older generation of owner/manager retires, becomes disabled, or dies. It also provides liquidity at a time when the entrepreneur's estate is usually entirely illiquid and tied up in the business. If properly drafted, it can solve one of the most difficult tax questions: the appropriate valuation of closely held business stock. Furthermore, if the buy-sell agreement is funded with insurance, it can provide significant funds for the entrepreneur's family at a small (and probably deductible) cost to the other members of the management group or the business itself.

Closely held businesses are often family businesses. The attorney can advise the client about the advantages derived from hiring family members and, if the business is organized in partnership form, about the pros and cons of the family partnership. The lawyer may also face the problem of dividing business interests upon divorce, or planning the estate of a business owner.

There is an important psychological component to effective business counseling. Tensions between family members, and especially between generations, are inescapable; part of the lawyer's role as counselor is to find ways to minimize these tensions without disrupting the business. For example, if a partnership form is not desirable, some family income-splitting may be possible through the use of Subchapter S.

Of course, once the business passes the "cottage-industry" stage, it will be necessary to employ nonfamily members. When that occurs, the lawyer has another role to play: educating the employer about tax withholding, Workers' Compensation, and possible liability under civil rights laws and laws dealing with unjust dismissal and occupational safety and health. Substantial savings may be possible through the use of independent contractors and/or leased employees; because this is a legal as well as an economic decision, the lawyer's input is valuable.

As for compliance, the business must avoid violations of laws dealing with air and water pollution, toxic waste, and product liability. Few members of the general or even business community are knowledgeable about the requirements of these laws: another educational and compliance task for the lawyer.

A final role the lawyer must play, and by no means the least important, is to give tax advice of the highest caliber. Sometimes the lawyer provides this advice; at other times, he or she works with the business's accountant or accountants. In either case, the business must pay a raft of taxes (from the obvious federal corporate tax to local taxes, which must be paid on time). The job of compliance is hard enough; the business also needs planning to minimize the future tax bite.

In short, the lawyer handling a business start-up has to play a variety of roles, from the most routine (filing routine papers) to the most sophisticated and technical (long-range tax planning; creating a compliance program). There is surprisingly little material written for the lawyer to explain to the conscientious business owner how to avoid wrongdoing or to the cautious business owner how to avoid liability. This portfolio will be a modest and pragmatic contribution to this end.

Business Start-up Practice is designed as, above all, a practical guide to the attorney advising a client who is contemplating starting a business. Our assumption is that the client seeks funding—probably by some combination of debt and equity—and that the business will be closely held at all times. We also assume that the business will be organized with an intention (perhaps delusional) of making a profit by actually producing some goods or providing a service, and thus will not be subject to special tax rules concerning tax shelters. The focus of this portfolio is on the pre-start-up and start-up period, not on the problems of the going business (e.g., commercial law). However, in some respects, the arrangements made during the start-up period will affect the entire course of the business. Because the attorney has the chance to set a firm foundation for good business practice, issues such as mechanisms for avoiding majority-minority conflict and various kinds of business liability are also discussed.

Contents

BUSINESS START-UP PRACTICE FLOW CHART

This Flow Chart shows the interactions between the legal and financial
aspects of business start-ups. The dotted lines connect corresponding parts
of the two processes.

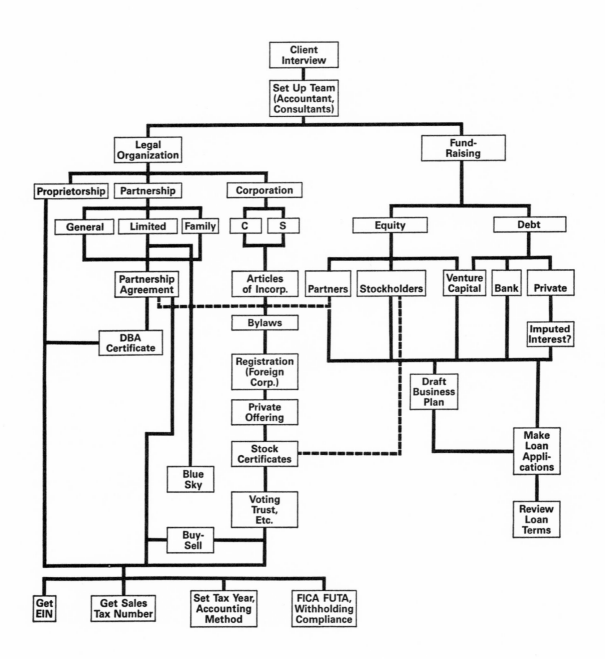

1

CLIENT INTERVIEWING AND RECORDKEEPING

At times, the most valuable service an attorney can do for the would-be entrepreneur is to convince him or her that the business idea is *not* a sound one and should be abandoned before a great deal of money is invested. Although the client is unlikely to be grateful at first, he or she may later realize that the lawyer's advice prevented a debacle.

When the business idea is better founded, the lawyer can help the client clarify the idea and give it legal form and expression. Anyone who starts a business is aware of the need for money, and has some idea of how the hoped-for profits will be divided; however, few clients are aware of such things as the subtleties of corporate law and the safeguards against squeeze-outs that can be built into a corporation's charter and bylaws. In addition, the client may have a long-range plan for business expansion, but have no plan for passing on the business to his or

1

her successor. If there is an estate plan, it may not include any meaningful provision for an interest in the business.

Once the business is set up, capitalized, and running, the lawyer can play a valuable advisory role. One of the lawyer's jobs is to "put out the fires": handle legal problems as they arise. Another role is to advise management about potential problems and things that could be done better. If the lawyer does an impressive job during the start-up phase, the business's owners are more likely to retain him or her as the need presents itself or on a continuing basis. Wouldn't you like to be the outside counsel to the firm that becomes the Xerox or the IBM of the twenty-first century? Maybe you can—if the founders of that future business giant come to you for advice on the start-up and *if* they're satisfied with your plan.

HOW TO WORK SUCCESSFULLY WITH A TEAM OF EXPERTS

It may be more helpful to think of the business start-up as a *team* rather than in terms of a single attorney handling all the work. Unless you're a CPA or have an extensive accounting background, it is a good idea first to recommend that the would-be entrepreneurs hire an accountant who is familiar with start-ups—and then work closely with him or her. Sometimes the client will either choose an alternative that is perfectly legal but has negative financial consequences (e.g., operating in partnership form when limited liability is desirable, using a conventional partnership when a family partnership would meet financial planning goals) or must choose among several possibilities (e.g., sources of capital), and can make a better decision if her or she understands the consequences for the business's income statement and balance sheet.

When Should You Consult a Legal Specialist?

At times it may be necessary for more than one attorney to be involved in the start-up. If, for example, you don't have a tax background, it may be appropriate to bring in a tax lawyer. If extensive securities work will be involved; if there are difficult intellectual property questions; if extensive and challenging questions of leasing, construction law, or other specialty areas arise in the course of the start-up, a legal specialist should be considered. Consulting a legal specialist is similar to a medical family practitioner consulting a kidney specialist about a patient suffering from kidney disease—sometimes it doesn't fall within your area of expertise. Remember, the most important factor is meeting your client's needs.

What if the client resists your suggestions, claiming that the extra legal expenses are too high? The client should then be reminded about the viability of the project and that since the projected business involves difficult legal issues, it should be capitalized so that funds are available for the necessary planning and preventive legal work.

Working With Other Professionals

Depending on the kind of business, other professionals may also be involved. Make sure that the client informs you who the other professionals will be—and work closely with them. Imagine the problems that would be incurred if the client's advertising agency plans a flamboyant (and expensive) campaign that is libelous or obscene, or that infringes on an established trademark or copyright, or that uses photographs taken without appropriate releases. Or, think what would happen to the award-winning restaurant design that has everything except an adequate number of exits, or that violates local health regulations or OSHA regulations.

ETHICAL PROBLEMS: WHO IS THE CLIENT?

That's a harder question than it seems. On the simplest level, the client is the person or group who approaches you (and pays your fee). But consider the fact that you may be counseling a group of people with clearly opposed interests. For example, you may be approached by three people who want to set up a partnership. Let's also say that they have enough sense to know that they need a partnership agreement. But should the agreement favor the service partners or the capital partner? A fifty-five-year-old partner will have an entirely different idea about the usefulness and preferred terms of a buy-sell agreement than a twenty-nine-year-old partner. How should the partnership's profits and losses be divided? Should the allocations for tax purposes be proportionate to capital contributions or allocated according to the partners' tax brackets?

Similarly, you might be retained by someone who wants to start a business in corporate form and who has lined up one or more investors. Should you draft the corporate instruments to favor the entrepreneur, or to protect the investors?

The perfect solution would be for each potential partner, stockholder-owner with management responsibilities, and potential nonmanaging investor to be represented by counsel. However, even if that option were not too expensive for most start-ups, the process of creating a new business would last almost forever because of the sheer difficulty of arranging liaison among all those lawyers.

A workable real-life solution is to advise the entire client group at the outset about the potential for conflict of interest; let them think about whether they need separate lawyers before you undertake the bulk of the work; and have them execute releases freeing you of the possibility of malpractice liability based on the "conflict of interest."

INTERVIEW CHECKLIST

The following are some of the questions you should ask the client in order to choose the optimum form of business organization and to draft the appropriate instruments for the new business:

Major Questions (Questions about overall structure and objectives)

1. What kind of business do you want to start?
2. How much money do you think it will take to start the business and keep it running until it begins to earn a profit?
3. How long do you think it will take to earn a profit?
4. Where do you plan to raise the capital for the business? How much control do you expect you will have to surrender to raise the capital?
5. Will you be starting this business by yourself, or do you have potential partners or stockholders?
6. How do you envision management responsibilities being allocated?
7. How will you support yourself and your family until the business is profitable?
8. How long are you prepared to hang on if the business encounters unexpected difficulties or takes longer than planned to become profitable?

Business Structure

(Questions about the legal form of operation.) *Note: It may be necessary to educate the clients about the various legal structures in order to get meaningful answers to the questions.*

1. Do you want to incorporate? Why?
2. If several people are involved, do you think a partnership or a corporation is the better form? Why?
3. If you want a partnership, would a family partnership be a wise idea? Why?
4. Are you interested in Sub S incorporation? Why?
5. Would you rate the business' liability exposure as low, moderate, or high? Why?
6. What are your personal assets which might be available to business creditors in an unincorporated business or in a nominal corporation if the corporate veil is pierced?
7. Are any relatives, friends, former employers, or potential clients willing to act as guarantors of business indebtedness?
8. Would it be simpler and more economical (in both financial and tax terms) to "start from scratch" or to acquire an existing business or business premises that have been converted for uses approximating those to which they will be put?
9. Should the business premises be rented, purchased outright in fee-simple form, or purchased in condominium form?

10. Will it be necessary to qualify as a foreign corporation in states in which you will be doing business and which are not the states of original incorporation?

Legal Structure

(Questions about legal problems that are likely to arise.)

1. Will the business involve patents, trademarks, copyrights, or other forms of regulated intellectual property? Have adequate searches been done to ensure that there will be no infringement? Have any necessary licenses been obtained, or at least are negotiations under way?

2. If purchasing a franchise is contemplated, have the required disclosure documents been obtained and submitted to a lawyer and/or accountant for examination?

3. If there will be any common-law employees, are you familiar with the requirements for withholding and depositing state and federal income taxes and FICA taxes? If there will be employees who receive tips, are you familiar with the special withholding procedure for tips? If there will be more than 15 common-law employees, are you aware of the mandates of Title VII and related anti-discrimination laws?

4. If a license is required for the business, can you qualify for the license?

5. Is the proposed business location suitable, given the relevant zoning, licensing, anti-pollution, and occupational safety laws?

Tax Structure

1. What would be the most favorable tax structure if the business were to encounter losses in the early years? Is this structure acceptable to potential co-entrepreneurs or investors?

2. What is the best debt-equity capitalization ratio from both the financial and tax viewpoints?

3. Is the proposed compensation for the original owner(s) "unreasonable" as defined by the IRS?

4. What is the appropriate ratio between immediate and deferred compensation? If the ratio calls for a great deal of deferred compensation, what contributions on behalf of rank-and-file employees will be mandated by ERISA and the tax code?

5. Which of the early expenses will be start-up expenses for tax purposes, and which will be ordinary and necessary expenses of doing business? Will start-up expenses be capitalized or amortized?

6. If the business is organized as a partnership, how should gains and losses be allocated? Are you familiar with the entity-level audit requirements for partnerships and S corporations?

7. Are you familiar with the state's franchise tax, corporate income tax, and/or unincorporated business tax?

Corporate (or Other) Organization

1. If cumulative voting is not mandated by the state of organization, is it a desirable feature?
2. Should the board of directors be classified?
3. Are transfer restrictions on the stock a good idea?
4. Is a buy-sell agreement useful to provide continuity for the enterprise while meeting the estate-planning needs of the founders? If so, what event(s) should trigger the buy-out: death, retirement, disability, dissension?
5. What protections for the minority owners are appropriate (e.g., super-majority requirements for certain important decisions, dissolution provisions, mandatory arbitration)?
6. How will conflicts among owners be handled (mandatory buy-out, mandatory arbitration, dissolution)?
7. What rights will stockholders have to inspect corporate books and records?
8. If the business is organized as a partnership, should provisions be made for continuation after an event that would cause statutory dissolution?
9. Are you familiar with the requirements for annual meetings, notice to stockholders, books and records, and minutes?
10. Who will serve as the incorporators and as the initial officers until the organizational meeting can be held?

Securities Considerations

1. Is par or no-par stock desired? Does the desired capitalization conform to state law?
2. Do you intend to issue both common and preferred stock? (If so, this will make a Subchapter S election impossible.)
3. Do you intend to issue both voting and nonvoting common? (This alternative can be combined with a Sub S election.)
4. How do you intend to sell the initial issue of stock? Do these plans conform to the federal exemptions from registration? Will it be necessary to "Blue Sky" the issue?
5. Do you intend to authorize stock that will not be issued immediately?

With these answers in hand, the attorney will know the kind of business the client intends to start and will be able to advise him or her on choosing the correct form of business. These answers will also tell you whether the client may run into other problems.

WHAT YOUR RECORDS SHOULD INCLUDE

In addition to the standard client intake forms and the answers to the questions above, the file on a business start-up should contain documents such as:

- A corporation's Articles of Incorporation (called Charter in some jurisdictions) and bylaws
- A corporation's Certificate of Incorporation or corresponding state-issued document creating the corporation as a legal entity
- Evidence of search of files for availability of the desired corporate name
- Pre-incorporation agreements (pp. 110–111)
- Disclosure documents from the franchisor (if the business is a franchise)
- Partnership agreements
- A "Doing Business As" (DBA) certificate for a noncorporate business utilizing an artificial name
- Contracts and correspondence relating to the acquisition or potential acquisition of a going business
- Commercial leases and/or documents involved in purchase of business real estate
- Documents relating to a Keogh or qualified pension plan
- Copies of voting agreements and/or voting trusts
- Copies of any required disclosure documents for issue of securities
- Copies of any union or employment contracts; copies of any documents that set out (or could be interpreted as setting out) business policies enforceable by employees

It will also be necessary to have a correspondence file and a record of telephone conversations plus any records needed in order to send out bills in a timely manner, or to substantiate that the terms of the retainer agreement are being complied with.

THE ROLES YOU MUST PLAY

Part of your job in a business start-up is to be a drafter: to create the documents needed to start a business and to keep it functioning. You must also be a counselor, advising the client about the many choices available. Another very important role is as an educator: you must teach the client about the laws that have to be complied with. You must also instruct the client about the requirements for annual meetings and corporate minutes; for trademark registration; for compliance with what seems like an endless supply of laws protecting the rights of employees and consumers; and for compliance with the UCC in both consumer and merchant transactions.

You may also be asked to sit on the new corporation's Board of Directors. Whether you should agree is an individual matter. However, be aware that it will be hard to be objective if you become part of the corporation's governing structure. Will your first allegiance be to maximize the corporation's profits, to represent the corporation zealously as an attorney, or to enforce the law? It's not impossible to do all three, but it certainly is difficult.

SETTING AND COLLECTING YOUR FEE

In order to get and keep the respect of a business client, it's important for the attorney to be businesslike. Business clients need and want clear agreements about what is to be done, on what timetable. These are the typical fee arrangements between attorneys and their business start-up clients:

• The attorney charges a flat fee for interviewing the client, giving the client some basic education about corporation and securities law, and preparing the Articles of Incorporation, bylaws, and shepherding the corporation through the incorporation process (if it is a corporation), or preparing a partnership agreement, DBA certificate, and giving the same kind of education to the partners of a business organized as a partnership. The attorney also makes the client aware of additional services available (e.g., qualification of the corporation as a foreign corporation; serving as the corporation's registered agent for service of process) and the fees for these services.

• An hourly fee. The key to success here is careful monitoring of *all* time spent on the matter, to capture the few minutes spent on a routine phone inquiry or item of correspondence. Those few minutes add up to potential billable hours over the course of the start-up process!

• An annual retainer, commencing with the business start-up process, and including routine legal services for a year. *PRACTICE TIP: The important thing here is to identify clearly which services are "routine," which are not covered by the agreement (e.g., protracted litigation) and must become the subject of separate negotiations.*

Certainly, your business clients should understand the value and importance of a written representation agreement. The agreement should include the following:

• A clear statement of exactly what you will do for the client.

• A workable timetable for these tasks, with an indication that the timetable is an estimate and actual scheduling may be different.

• Specific authority for you to act on your client's behalf.

• A waiver of potential conflict-of-interest claims, if you represent several persons starting a business, if their interests could be adverse (e.g., you draft bylaws that are, in effect, more favorable to one client than to the others).

• An explicit formula for determining your compensation.

• An explanation of your billing practices. *PRACTICE TIP: Some lawyers charge interest on overdue bills. When the client is a consumer, charging interest usually mobilizes the entire federal Truth in Lending apparatus of law and regulations. Although this is not true for business clients, it is still worthwhile to make full disclosure of the amount of interest payable, and conditions under which it will be charged.*

• An explanation of your file retention policies. It's important to go through your files periodically and to eliminate unnecessary duplicate copies in active files, to move materials to "dead" files, and to return "dead" files that will not be needed (e.g., matters on which no litigation is involved and on which the statute of limitations on hypothetical claims has expired) to the client. Your representation agreement should make it clear that such materials will be returned to the client.

• If possible, include an item that states that bills for your services and for cost disbursements must be handled promptly—not subjected to the business' usual bill-paying cycle. This addition could get a check to you a month or so faster than if you get the same treatment as ordinary vendors.

EXAMPLE: Let's say that you handled the incorporation process for Spinks and Jencks, Inc. The founders, Edward Spinks and Martha Jencks, are impressed by your work and have placed you on annual retainer to handle routine legal work. Your representation agreement should make it clear that the retainer rate quoted is guaranteed only for a certain amount of time—either for one full year or until the end of the current year. Otherwise, you could find yourself representing a successful corporation, when you're a successful practitioner—at a minimal rate set when you were both starting out, and never reviewed since.

It's important to review your retainer rates every year, and to check the rates against both your time and effort expended, and against the actual benefits provided to the client. It can be a good business practice to *refund* part of the retainer in a year when you have performed little or no actual work for the client. On the other hand, don't do involuntary "pro bono" work: if a retainer leaves no room for profit once your hours and overhead are taken into account, either the rate must be raised or you must substitute other, more profitable work for representing that particular client.

No client ever pays before the fee is requested! This is especially true of start-up businesses, with their typical poor cash flow and surplus of other bills to pay. So be sure that your bills are:

• Rendered regularly—at least quarterly, preferably monthly, unless the client is an annual retainer client. In that case, make sure that a substantial portion of the retainer is paid on account. Clients don't feel grateful for services they can barely remember.

• Neat and businesslike in appearance; fully detailed. There's an old maxim in the law: "If the law is against you, pound the facts; if the facts are against you, pound the law. If both are against you, pound the table!" This also applies to billing. If you were forced to spend a lot of hours on a frustrating negotiation or looking for ultimately unavailable information, stress the number of hours spent and exactly how much time was required for each task.

On the other hand, you might have spent a short amount of time drafting a document that's routine for you, but of crucial importance to the client. In that case, stress the value of the work to the client by presenting a detailed bill, heavy in "action words," showing that your services have been both many and valuable.

EXAMPLE: Held conference with E. Spinks and M. Jencks. Discussed their personal financial resources and needs. Reviewed applicable state and federal laws to devise a corporate structure suitable for founders' and business' needs. Drafted Articles of Incorporation as statutory close corporation. Prepared bylaws, buy-sell agreement, employment contracts for principal executives (copies attached). Researched availability of desired corporate name. Ordered corporate kit (see attached invoice for disbursement). Carried out procedures mandated by state law for incorporation of statutory close corporation. (See attached copy of official Certificate of Incorporation.)

PRACTICE TIP: Periodic billing is also a way to inform clients of what has been done on their behalf and to reassure them that you are performing the work conscientiously and efficiently. Frequently, clients are unaware just how much work goes into a routine transaction; awareness increases their willingness to pay promptly. Submitting copies of relevant documents with the bill further reinforces the client's understanding of what you've done and how much has been completed.

Once you've determined who the real client is, have resolved any possible conflicts of interest and have set the terms on which you will represent the client(s), it's time to determine the form under which the new business will be conducted, and take the practical and legal steps to set it up. Good planning at the outset can eliminate or minimize legal, practical, and financial problems later on, and can arrange a smooth transition to a new owner or a new generation of owners. Good planning can also maximize the after-tax wealth of the business's owners, allow them to retire comfortably, and allow them to pass on their interest in the business and their other assets to their designated heirs, at the minimum allowable estate and transfer tax cost.

This book is based on the following assumptions about the business start-ups you'll be counseling (other kinds of business start-ups will not be addressed here):

• The business is set up with the intention of making a profit, sooner or later. Although the intention may never be fulfilled, the purpose *is* to make money by manufacturing or providing services; not to create a tax shelter (although investors may be interested in early losses as a tax shelter) or to serve as a not-for-profit corporation.

- The business will at least commence operations as a closely held business, though it may eventually go public.

- There will be a comparatively small number of managers, all of whom will probably be stockholders.

- If there are common-law employees, they will not be unionized, and no move to unionize will be made during the start-up period.

- The business is organized either as a proprietorship, general partnership, limited partnership, C corporation, or S corporation—that is, not as a joint venture or business trust.

- If the business is a corporation, it will be incorporated in the state in which its operations are centralized; it may also qualify as a foreign corporation in one or more other states.

- The entire capitalization will come either from a single entrepreneur, from partners, from stockholders, or from loans (private or from lending institutions): no bonds, hybrid instruments, or other complex forms of financing will be used.

2

CHOOSING THE BUSINESS FORM

One of the most fundamental decisions you will have to make is the choice of legal entity for operating the business. Most clients will want to operate the business in corporate form, though this is not necessarily the best choice. It may be better to commence operations as a proprietorship or partnership, later incorporating the business as financial and tax considerations change.

In addition to the client's preference, there are several factors in the choice of business form:

- Ease of creating and maintaining the entity
- Conformity between the form of the business and its actual management and financial structure
- Maximization of after-tax income
- Simplicity of accounting

- Ease of transferring assets and interests in the business
- Prevention of undesired transfers of assets and interests in the business
- Continuity and transition to a new generation of owners
- Wealth-building for the business owners and their families
- Ease of raising new capital as needed
- Maximization of benefits available to the owners (without incurring a ruinous obligation to provide corresponding benefits for employees)
- Limitation of personal liability of owners
- Degree of regulation to which the business operation and its owners will be subjected

Because these factors differ from business to business (and from time to time, within a given business), there is no one optimum form. The rate of failure for new businesses is very high, so the various forms must be assessed for their "escape" potential as well as their potential for helping a going business succeed.

PROPRIETORSHIP

Sole proprietorship is the simplest—one might say the primal—form of business. The entrepreneur is sole owner (though he or she may be indebted to various persons and organizations who extend credit to the business) and is solely responsible for all business obligations. The proprietor's personal assets can be reached for business debts and for tort judgments arising out of business operations.

The proprietorship has no continuity of existence; it ceases to exist when the proprietor dies or simply abandons the business. The proprietorship's assets and good will can be sold, but then they become someone else's business.

The tax consequences of proprietorship can be quite negative, because the proprietor's taxable income includes all the business' profits, whether or not he or she takes any or all of the profits out of the business in the form of a salary or reinvests some or all of the profits in business expansion. On the other hand, a proprietorship can be a welcome source of tax losses to an otherwise high-bracket taxpayer.

A proprietorship can be entered into (and exited from) quite simply; with few or no formalities. If the business is of a sort mandating a license, the license must of course be obtained; and if the proprietorship will be operated under an artificial name, a DBA certificate must be obtained. Otherwise, the business can be started quickly and ceased at any time as long as the proprietorship's debts are paid. There is little regulation of proprietorships. The proprietor is the sole decision maker; there are no stockholders to mollify, no Board of Directors to persuade.

To sum up, the proprietorship excels in simplicity, inexpensiveness of creation, and flexibility of operations. Its disadvantages are unlimited liability (which can be controlled to some extent by acquiring adequate liability insurance against reasonably foreseeable risks) and the potential tax liability in excess of the cash taken out of the business. The proprietor is not eligible for participation in a qualified pension plan or for various other employee benefits that a corporate executive or shareholder-employee would be eligible for. However, a sole proprietor is entitled to set aside substantial sums by establishing a Keogh plan, especially a defined-benefit Keogh.

EXAMPLE: I own a business in proprietorship form. I'm disappointed by the business's lack of dramatic success; but, as sole owner, investor, and "employee," I'm pleased by the ease with which I was able to cancel the New York DBA certificate and get a New Jersey DBA certificate as soon as I moved the business (and the crate after crate of plain English forms) to New Jersey. The accounting and tax chores are simplicity itself.

PARTNERSHIP

Frequently, several people will be associated in a business enterprise. They may have overlapping tasks and make equal contributions to the partnership's capital or, one may contribute technical skills, another business skills, yet others have money to invest.

Such a group has several alternatives; a partnership is the traditional one. A general partnership, like a proprietorship, is an unlimited liability form; furthermore, each partner's assets can be reached without limitation for partnership obligations incurred by the other partners (perhaps contrary to the partner's wishes). Partnership creditors do not have to attempt to collect from the various partners proportionate to their interest in the partnership capital or partnership profits—all of the debt can be collected from any one of the partners.

A partnership is limited in duration. Technically, a partnership dissolves whenever a partner dies, becomes disabled, or withdraws from the partnership; in order to keep the business in operation, provisions must be made via partnership agreement.

In the absence of partnership agreement provisions to the contrary, a partner will be taxed on his or her proportional share of partnership profits, not on his or her draw from the partnership. The partnership agreement may provide to the contrary: partnership profits (and, perhaps more important to high-bracket partners, partnership losses) may be allocated differently. As long as the allocation reflects economic reality (e.g., contributions of a service partner are taken into account), the IRS will abide by the allocation. *PRACTICE TIP: Absent a provision in the partnership agreement to the contrary, the IRS will divide profits proportionately. This is not necessarily true of state taxes; New York, for instance, allocates profits in equal shares absent a provision in the partnership agreement.*

A partnership, like a proprietorship, is not a taxpayer. However, a partnership, unlike a proprietorship, must file an information return with the IRS annually. Current IRS practice calls for audits at the partnership level, and requires all partners to treat the items of profit and loss passed through to them in a fashion consistent with the partnership's information return. That is, if there are five partners, it is not acceptable for each of them to claim 35% of a tax loss or credit.

Again, like proprietorships, partnerships provide the possibility of Keogh plans for the partners, but preclude qualified pension plans and fringe benefits available to corporate employees. Yet another similarity: interests in general partnerships, like interests in proprietorships, are quite difficult to transfer because there is no ready market for them. A proprietor can do whatever he or she likes with the business (within the bounds of the law); a partner must abide by the wishes of his or her partners to a greater or lesser extent (depending on whether there is a partnership agreement, and what it says).

A general partnership, in many ways, is like a marriage. Given good faith and compatability, a partnership can be outstandingly successful. However, there must be open channels of communication between the partners (in either situation), and divorce is not uncommon in either situation.

Some marital partners find antenuptial agreements helpful. The partnership equivalent—the partnership agreement—is not legally mandated, but should be considered a practical requisite of the formation of every general partnership. The partnership agreement should address issues such as:

- Capital to be contributed by each partner
- Amount of time each partner will contribute to the affairs of the partnership; limitations on competition with the partnership
- Extent to which further capital contributions can be demanded, and on what terms
- Share of partnership profits each partner is entitled to, and when it will be paid out
- The "draw" each partner is entitled to take, pending periodic settlements
- Allocation of partnership losses
- Buy-sell provisions (see pages 83–84)
- Continuity after technical dissolution
- Which partner will be the "audit partner" required by the IRS
- Procedure for resolving disagreement among the partners

To sum up, a partnership is a limited duration, unlimited liability form of business. It can be created very simply, as a "handshake" deal, although it is much more prudent to have a well-drafted partnership agreement. Government regulation of partnerships is limited: various licenses may have to be obtained for the business itself, and a DBA certificate will be required if an artificial name is used, but no permission or authority is required to create the partnership itself.

Partnerships can create extremely difficult problems of management, if partners disagree among themselves and if lines of command are not clear. In such a situation, it is not uncommon for one or more partners to force dissolution of the partnership at a time disadvantageous for business operations or for the financial and/or tax postures of the other partners. If a partner wants to leave the partnership and get his or her capital back and the other partners are unwilling to buy him or her out, there are few outside buyers interested in purchasing the partnership interest (and admission of a new partner is, in any case, subject to the veto power of the existing partners).

Partnerships also require sophisticated (and potentially expensive) tax accounting, both to prepare the partnership's books, records, and information returns, and to inform the partners of changes in the basis of their partnership interests and their allocations of profit and loss.

Limited Partnerships

The limited partnership is a legal device that allows would-be investors in a partnership business to avoid some of the disadvantages of the general partnership form. A limited partnership must have at least one general partner, who (or which—a corporation or partnership can be the general partner) remains liable without limitation.

The limited partners, however, are mere passive investors. They do not have management powers; in return, they are protected against unlimited liability. (However, a limited partner can be an employee of the partnership or can render professional services to the partnership, without being treated as a general partner.) They can lose their entire investment in the partnership, but their other assets cannot be reached by partnership creditors. In a sense, the limited partnership can be conceptualized as a hybrid between the general partnership and the corporation: limited partners are more or less analogous to stockholders, although their tax position is different. Like stockholders, and unlike general partners, limited partners can transfer their interest in the partnership freely. They are entitled to pass-through of partnership tax items such as deductions and tax credits; however, limited partners are likely to be "passive investors" as defined by the tax code of 1986, and thus can use losses only to offset other passive income, not active income such as employee compensation.

Partnerships existed at common law, but the limited partnership is a creature of statute. Forty-nine states have adopted either the Uniform Limited Partnership Act or the Revised Uniform Limited Partnership Act, the 1976 draft. (Louisiana, ever creative in statutory matters, has a form called the "partnership in commendam" which is roughly equivalent to limited partnership.)

Therefore, creation of a limited partnership must comply with the applicable state statute. Limited partnership interests may also be "securities" as defined by the relevant Blue Sky Law, so registration and/or some form of disclosure may be required. Also check the relevant statute to see if the name of the partnership must be reserved (as a corporate name may have to be reserved—see page 114), and once an official certificate of limited partnership has been issued, whether publication of the certificate in one or more newspapers is required. [See, New York Partnership Law §91(b).]

Proprietorships and general partnerships can do business in states other than the states of their original creation, without registration or permission from the other states. As you'll see below, foreign corporations must register in order to do business in states other than their state(s) of incorporation. The status of foreign limited partnerships is more ambiguous. Arkansas, Connecticut, Maryland, Minnesota, Washington, West Virginia, and Wyoming have adopted Article 9 of the Revised Uniform Limited Partnership Act, and therefore have registration and choice-of-law rules for foreign limited partnerships. Eleven states have statutes regulating foreign limited partnerships (e.g., by requiring filing of the original partnership certificate, paying a fee, and appointing an in-state agent for service of process). The states and cites are as follows:

CAL Corp. Code §15700; FLA §§620.40-.49; HAW §425-77; IDA §53-306(2); KAN §56-123(b), (c); KY §362.095; ME T31 §181; NH §§305-A;1—A:8; NY Partnership Article 8-A; ORE §§69.440,.450; TEX Laws 1977 ch. 408 §§32, 1107-8.

In the other thirty-two states, both drafters and potential limited partners should be careful; it can't be guaranteed that the limitation on liability will be observed if the limited partnership is doing business outside the original state of its creation.

Family Partnerships

The partnership form is attractive to high-bracket investors when the partnership is losing money; they get to avail themselves of loss deductions. However, if capital is a material income-producing factor in the partnership, that is it is not a pure personal-service business such as a partnership formed by several entertainers or management consultants, and if the partnership is profitable enough to make tax planning imperative for the partners, the "family partnership" as defined by Section 704 of the Code may be an attractive tax planning device for the partners. The IRS may take a more cynical view of the role of capital than most people would: e.g., *U.S. v. Van Dyke*, 696 F.2d 957 (Fed.Cir. 1982) [capital was not an income-producing factor in a taxidermy business with $100,000 worth of equipment and 20 employees]. Where capital is not an income producing factor, incorporating as an S corporation will permit family income-splitting but a family partnership will not.

The family partnership permits shifting of income to other family members (presumably with lower tax brackets) by donating partnership interests to them. Income thrown off by the partnership interest will be taxed to the new owner, not to the donor. This is true whether or not the donee of the partnership interest is a minor, and whether or not service is or could be rendered to the partnership. However, the "kiddie tax" provisions of the Tax Code of 1986 must be considered.

However, the partnership's counsel should be aware of (and should inform the clients about) the effect of Reg. §1.704-1(e)(3)(i)(b): before income is allocated to a donated family partnership interest, reasonable compensation for the donor of the interest must first be deducted. Furthermore, the share of income allocated to the donee can't be greater than that allocated to the donor's remaining capital interest in the partnership.

It's possible that a partnership is the optimum choice for a start-up business but later, as the business becomes successful, it is no longer a practical or tax-wise form of operation. This is because there may no longer be delectable write-offs; even using the family partnership device, the partners may have an inconvenient amount of taxable income (especially if they have a poor cash flow because they devote much of the partnership profits to expansion). Luckily, Code Section 351 permits tax-free incorporation of a partnership (or proprietorship) under certain circumstances; an unwise choice of form, or a wise choice rendered inconvenient by changed circumstances, is neither fatal nor final. (A taxable corporation may be the better choice if the new corporation wants a stepped-up basis in the business assets.) Incorporation of a going business is discussed on pages 36–37.

However, some businesses (and some business owners) are better suited to immediate incorporation. Incorporation offers some enormous advantages, offset by enormous risks. The attorney's job is to use planning and drafting to offset the risks and maximize the advantages.

CORPORATIONS

The enormous advantages of incorporation can be summed up as indefinite existence and limited liability. Unless the "corporate veil" has been pierced (see pages 69–72), stockholders can lose their entire investment in corporate stock, but cannot be held responsible for corporate debts or liabilities in excess of their investment. Given the possibility of multibillion-dollar judgments against corporations, this is indeed a blessing.

Furthermore, corporate stock is, at least theoretically, freely transferrable. The "theoretically" comes in because the market for stock in small, closely held businesses is limited; because such stock may be covered by transfer restrictions (see pages 84–85); and because sales of stock must be made either after a difficult and expensive registration process or in strict compliance with the exemptions from registration (see page 44). And, although there is some trading in limited partnership interests, in practice, the corporate form is the only one that gives the initial owners of the business the chance to make a lot of money by "taking the company public."

The enormous disadvantages can be summed up as a need for formalities; a strong possibility of double taxation; and the almost certain conflict between majority and minority shareholders, with concomitant possibilities for squeeze outs on one side, blocking corporate progress on the other.

In order to exist as a valid corporation, certain formalities in both creation and management must be observed. The corporation must have Articles of Incorporation. Capital must be paid in exchange for shares. An organization meeting must be held; bylaws must be adopted. An initial Board of Directors must either be named in the Articles of Incorporation or elected at the organization meeting (this depends on individual state law; some states give the business founders a choice). There must be annual meetings of stockholders and of directors. Minutes must be taken. The corporation must have certain officers, as detailed in the state statute.

Of course, there's something a bit absurd about a business started by two or three people (or a single person) holding frequent meetings for the purpose of electing themselves to the Board of Directors and naming themselves officers. To address this problem, and also the ubiquitous majority-minority conflicts, a number of states have adopted "statutory close corporation" provisions (more about this on page 25). These range from straightforward statements permitting shareholders to make valid agreements about corporate governance without running afoul of the normal requirement that a corporation be managed by its Board of Directors, to permission to eliminate the Board of Directors entirely and have the corporation run by its shareholders, to lengthy integrated statutes dealing with close corporation governance and transfer restrictions.

For many business owners, the risk of double taxation is the greatest obstacle to incorporation. The corporation, as an artificial person, is a very real taxpayer. It pays taxes on its own income, after taking into account its income items, deductions, and credits. If it encounters losses, they are carried forward to affect the corporation's own tax return, and are not passed through to the stockholders. Then, whatever portion of after-tax income is paid out in dividends is taxed again in the hands of the stockholders who receive the dividends. In many states, corporations are also subject to franchise and/or income taxes. (Such taxes are more common than corresponding taxes on unincorporated businesses, but unincorporated business taxes are not unheard of—the practitioner must consult secondary sources such as the *CCH State Tax Guide* and the state and local statutes.)

The Subchapter S ("S") corporation, a creation of the Internal Revenue Code, solves many of these problems. The S corporation, like an ordinary ("C") corporation, can have perpetual duration. Its stockholders are entitled to the protection of limited liability. But the S corporation is a pass-through entity, and is not a taxpayer. An information return, but no tax return, is filed for the S corporation; items of income, loss, deduction, and credit pass through to the stockholders and are taken into account on their returns.

The S Corporation

Treatment as an S corporation is not automatic; the corporation must make an election to be an S corporation. The election need not be made as soon as the corporation starts up (it can't be made before the state of incorporation issues the Certificate of Incorporation officially starting the corporate existence—Letter Ruling 8530100). It's permissible for the corporation to begin its existence as a C corporation, then elect later—but this would require the creation of two different accounting systems. As a result of the Tax Code of 1986, gain may also have to be recognized on the changeover. So it's easier all around for the practitioner to advise clients on the pros and cons of Sub S before the incorporation process begins, and to draft the Articles of Incorporation and any permissible and desirable transfer restrictions (see pages 84–85) with this in mind.

To qualify for the S election, a corporation must:

- be a domestic corporation
- not be ineligible for the election: companies that are members of an affiliated group of corporations, some insurance companies and financial institutions, and former Domestic International Sales Corporations (DISCs) are ineligible by statute
- have 35 or fewer stockholders; however, a married couple both of whom own stock are treated as a single stockholder, and so is a voting trust
- not have any ineligible stockholders: individuals, estates, and voting trusts are allowed to own Sub S stock, but many other trusts and nonresident aliens are not permitted
- have only one "class" of stock

The "one class" requirement could be a problem for corporations that want to issue preferred stock (for example, to permit transfer of control from older to younger generations in the founding family). If preferred stock is a "must" in the initial capitalization, Sub S will just have to be forgone; if it won't be needed until later, the company can start up as an S corporation and become a C corporation later in its operations.

It is permissible for an S corporation to issue both voting and nonvoting common stock; the two issues will not be considered to be separate classes of stock as long as they have identical rights in the corporation's profits and assets. Nor will "straight debt" be considered a second class of stock if it falls within the following "safe harbor" rules:

- the debt is evidenced by a written, unconditional obligation to pay the debt, either on a specific schedule or on demand
- a variable interest rate is permissible—as long as the interest rate depends on external factors such as the prime rate, not on corporate income or profits (because that would put the alleged creditor in the position of a stockholder)
- the debt instruments are not convertible to stock
- the creditor would be eligible to be a shareholder in the S corporation

The "one class of stock" requirement has been litigated fairly often, and has been the subject of a number of IRS letter rulings and Revenue Rulings. Consider, for example, Rev.Rul.85-161, IRB 1985-41 p. 22. The S corporation in question had both voting and nonvoting common; the agreement restricting the transfer of an officer's nonvoting common stock did not create a second class of stock. The agreement, a fairly conventional transfer-restrictions agreement (see page 98) required the consent of all the owners of voting common stock in order to sell the nonvoting common. If consent was not forthcoming, the stock could be sold only to the corporation or other stockholders at its book value; either the corporation or the other stockholders could buy out the officer's interest on death, disability, or termination of employment with the corporation. Letter Ruling 8423049 is similar: a stock purchase agreement between an S corporation and a key employee, providing that the employee has to sell his stock back to the firm if the majority stockholder ever sold more than half of his stock, did not create a second class of stock.

The corporation itself makes the election, on IRS Form 2553, but everyone who is a shareholder on the day of the election must indicate consent. If any stock is held jointly, both spouses must consent. The consents can either be made on the Form 2553 or on a separate statement attached to the election form, giving:

- the shareholder's name, address, and taxpayer identification number
- the number of shares he or she holds in the corporation
- the date or dates on which they were acquired
- an indication of consent
- a signature

The election for any taxable year must either be made in the preceding taxable year (which is impossible, for a start-up corporation) or on or before the fifteenth day of the third month of the tax year [Code §1362(b)]. If the first tax year has less than two months and fifteen days, the election is effective for that year if it's made within the first two months and fifteen days.

In general, an S corporation must have either a calendar year or a fiscal year impelled by a valid business purpose. Under the Tax Code of 1986, the taxable year of an S corporation should conform to the owners' taxable years; and use of a particular year based on hiring patterns, financial accounting, or administrative purposes will no longer be considered a valid business purpose.

Corporations electing Sub S and also choosing a fiscal year must file an additional statement with their Form 2553, indicating that they've complied with the terms of Rev.Proc. 83-25, 1983-1 CB 689, and indicating which acceptable motivation has led them to choose the fiscal year.

S corporations are indeed corporations for pension and benefit purposes, and Keogh plans are unavailable. An S corporation is allowed to have a profit-sharing plan if contributions are keyed to profits as determined by generally accepted accounting principles, even though the amounts involved are actually taxed to the stockholders and are not "accumulated profits" for federal income tax purposes (Rev.Rul. 80-252, 1980-2 CB 130).

EXAMPLE: Peter Roffman is an inventor who has devised a new type of coffee-maker that he believes is patentable. His friend, William Martin, has funds to invest; William Martin's daughter, Christine O'Toole, has an MBA and wants to work part time until her two-year-old son starts school.

After interviewing all three, you determine that William Martin is especially interested in limitation of his financial liability—he understands that, since his is the "deep pocket," creditors of the new business will look to him first. Since neither Roffman nor O'Toole has much in the way of assets, he also knows that it would be difficult to look to them for reimbursement if the business were organized in partnership form.

Therefore, you determine that the business should be a corporation; tax factors favor the use of the Subchapter S corporation. There are no securities law problems, because the three founders are the only stockholders. However, because Sub S stock may not be issued for *future* services, both Roffman and O'Toole insist on employment contracts specifying the conditions under which stock will later be issued to them after they have rendered services to the corporation.

The outcome of the discussion is that they decide to incorporate immediately, taking the risks that the new coffee-maker will not be patentable and that the business will be unsuccessful if the new design must be sold without patent protection. In their judgment, the comparatively small costs of incorporation are a worthwhile investment in order to be able to "take off" as soon as the coffee-makers can be produced commercially.

You also refer the three founders to a law school classmate of yours who is a leading patent attorney, so they can find out if the technology is patentable, and to undertake the patent process if it is. While he's at work, you research the legal implications of a licensing agreement with a major appliance manufacturer, and review the lease for the factory space and the contracts with suppliers of raw materials.

Business Planning Under the Tax Code of 1986

The impact of the new Code is far-reaching, and it'll take several years to sort it all out. However, some effects can already be anticipated, as follows:

• Partnerships may become less attractive; partners who do not participate actively in management of the business will be subject to the new Code's rules on "passive activities." Although partners will be fully taxed on income, they will only be allowed to use passive losses to offset passive income (e.g., stock dividends)— passive losses cannot be used to shelter active income such as salary. Furthermore, if a closely held corporation has passive losses itself, such losses can be used to offset active business income but not portfolio income.

• As a result of changes in tax brackets, and the elimination of the capital gains preference, a corporation may be paying tax at a higher rate than its stockholder-employees—therefore, the strategy of retaining income within the corporation in the hope of deriving tax-favored capital gains on the stock's appreciation may become less attractive.

• The old strategy called for key employees to press for a great deal of deferred compensation, expecting to be in a lower bracket at post-retirement. The new, "flatter" rate structure makes this strategy obsolete; executives will probably demand higher current income (so the business may need more cash).

Major changes in tax accounting (new rules about fiscal years, FIFO, and the cash method) are discussed elsewhere in this Portfolio.

Professional Corporations

Today, to most lawyers, the abbreviation "PC" stands for the small computer churning out billings and (if he or she is imaginative) aiding drafting. A few years ago, the abbreviation would probably have been interpreted to mean "Professional Corporation."

All the states except West Virginia have statutes dealing with the Professional Corporation (sometimes called the Professional Association). The PC or PA, like a business corporation, can have perpetual duration, without the necessity for special continuation provisions that partnerships encounter.

However, unlike a business corporation, the PC is not entirely a limited-liability form. The member-stockholders of the PC (all of whom must be licensed members of the profession being practiced in corporate form) retain full liability for their own acts of negligence, professional misconduct, and malpractice. (But, depending on the state and the terms of the Articles of Incorporation and agreements among the stockholders, it may be possible to limit liability for such acts committed by other members of the PC.)

There's case law to the effect that PC shareholders can be made personally liable for the PC's bad checks [*First Bank and Trust Co. v. Zagoria*, 250 Ga. 844, 302 SE2d 674 (1983)] and unpaid rent [*South High Development Ltd. v. Weiver, Lippe & Gormley Co., CPA*, 4 Oh.St.3d 1, 445 NE2d 1106 (1983)]. TIP: Advise the client to make it clear on the letterhead and on all communications that the professional organization carries on its business in PC form—this may at least induce creditors to approach the PC first for payment rather than assuming the professionals are partners and approaching them as individual debtors.

Furthermore, since all shareholders must be members of the profession, the PC device can't be used to raise capital for the professional enterprise from outsiders. This fact makes a buy-sell agreement returning each professional's stock to the corporation on his or her death, retirement, or loss of license especially imperative.

One of the major reasons for incorporating professional practices was the pre-1982 distinction between retirement plans available to corporations and the Keogh plans available to unincorporated business and professional practices. Under current law, the gap has narrowed (although there are some respects in which qualified plans are more generous to highly compensated employees than Keogh plans are). Furthermore, the new laws affecting top-heavy pension plans (and most small plans are top-heavy, because the total number of participants, and the ratio of support staff to highly compensated employees, are so small) make it difficult for PC members to grant themselves substantial retirement benefits without corresponding generosity to common-law employees.

Therefore, PCs have become much less attractive—indeed, Prentice-Hall, Inc. discontinued supplementation of its two-volume Professional Corporations

looseleaf service in 1983, because the development of new law and new incorpora-
tions of professional practice had slowed to a crawl.

However, if you do have a client contemplating incorporation of a professional practice, check the state cites given in the table on pages 114–115. There may
still be advantages derived from incorporation of the practice or of incorporation
of individual practitioners and forming a partnership among the various PCs.

What happens if conflicts among PC professionals are impairing service to
clients? One alternative, permitted by Letter Ruling 8544050, is to have a
nontaxable reorganization and spinoff by transferring assets to a new professional
corporation in exchange for the new corporation's shares, then exchanging the
withdrawing professional's shares for shares in the new corporation. The net effect
is that the dissenter has his or her own corporation to play with.

Statutory Close Corporations

Theoretically, all corporations are closely held until they meet the qualifications required to sell their shares to the public. In practice, there are real
differences between the dynamics of a corporation owned by thousands or millions
of shareholders who see the corporation only as a potential source of dividends
and capital gains and a corporation owned by a handful of initial investors who
take a lively interest in corporate management, and many of whom are on the
payroll. (In fact, one of the most difficult issues in the close corporation is
resolving the conflict between stockholder-employees, who want much of the
corporate resources to be devoted to improved compensation for employees and
long-term growth, and the other stockholders, who want a stream of current
dividend income.)

Similarly, the formalities required to govern a corporation with billions of
dollars in assets and a largely anonymous horde of stockholders are quite
inappropriate for a company consisting of Cousins Izzy and Moe, and Moe's
daughter Bernice who types the invoices.

Therefore, several states have adopted integrated close corporation statutes.
(The cites are in the table of statutes.) Arizona's statute, for instance, limits a close
corporation to ten stockholders (married couples count as a single stockholder),
and requires the Articles of Incorporation to state that the corporation is close; to
disclose the names, addresses, and the initial contributions of the stockholders.
The Arizona close corporation is managed by "managers," not a Board of
Directors; their names and addresses must be disclosed in the Articles of
Incorporation, and they must give the stockholders an annual accounting unless
the Articles of Incorporation exempt them from this task.

California and Minnesota close corporations may have up to 35 stockholders—again, married couples (and trusts) count as only one.

Under Delaware law, a close corporation can have up to 30 shareholders; it
cannot make a public offering of stock; and may, if it wishes, specify in its
Certificate of Incorporation who is qualified or excluded from owning its stock.

Furthermore, its stock *must* be subject to transfer restrictions—for example, restrictions to preserve Sub S status, to require would-be sellers to give an option to fellow stockholders, and the like. A Delaware close corporation's shareholders can provide for management by the shareholders rather than a Board of Directors—at the cost, of course, of assuming the liability the directors are normally subject to. The Illinois, Kansas, Pennsylvania, and Wisconsin acts are similar.

A Maine close corporation can have up to 20 shareholders (whether or not they have voting rights), and the Articles of Incorporation must include the words, "There shall be no directors initially; the shares of the corporation will not be sold to more than 20 persons; the business of the corporation will be managed by the shareholders."

The attorney handling the start-up of a close corporation in a state without a comprehensive close corporation law should examine the local law closely. Most state corporation statutes require a certain number of directors or officers; many state laws require at least two officers, because the offices of President and Secretary cannot be held by the same person. But some statutes allow the number of directors to equal the number of stockholders and permit any number of offices to be held by a single person. If this is not permitted, the logically offensive result is that outsiders must be chosen for high corporate office, because the supply of insiders is inadequate.

THE INCORPORATION PROCESS

The process of incorporating a new business involves a number of steps and technicalities. To many business owners—and to many attorneys—these steps are seen as mere formalities, to be handled by routine adoption of a number of forms.

Although there is an element of this in the incorporation process, the pre-incorporation stage provides a chance for the drafter to create a corporate structure that will function smoothly, provide optimum financial and tax results for participants, and minimize (nothing will eliminate) majority-minority conflicts.

The Articles of Incorporation and bylaws can be absolutely routine documents, containing nothing but the least controversial boilerplate provisions. But state corporation statutes give corporations a good deal of latitude in drafting these documents, and they can be used to enlarge the corporate powers, provide flexibility that may be needed in later years, and alter the balance of power among the stockholders and between the group of stockholders and the officers and directors.

The drafter must also be aware of idiosyncratic state requirements in the incorporation process. For instance, Arizona §10-128 requires the Articles of Incorporation to be accompanied by a sworn disclosure statement indicating whether any officer, director, or 10% stockholder has ever been found guilty of a securities violation, consumer fraud, or related offenses. Several states (Arizona,

Georgia, Iowa, and Nebraska) require publication of the Articles themselves or of a notice of incorporation.

The states have elaborate procedures for amending or restating the Articles of Incorporation, so initial mistakes can be corrected (if the balance of power in corporate politics permits). Still, it is better to do it right the first time. The drafter must educate the client about issues such as the various kinds of securities that can be issued (voting common; nonvoting common; preferred, cumulative or not; series and classes of shares; treasury shares; convertible bonds; rights, options, and warrants), and about important corporate law issues such as cumulative voting, preemptive rights, supermajority voting requirements, and transfer restrictions (to be discussed later in this chapter). If the state recognizes the statutory close corporation, the Articles of Incorporation will probably have to indicate that the corporation elects such treatment.

Steps in the Process

The start-up of a corporation will include some or all of the following steps (not necessarily in this order):

- A client conference to find out what the clients want and the best ways to attain their objectives; modifying objectives if necessary in light of corporation, tax, and securities law.
- Choosing incorporators. In most states, any adult, corporation, or partnership can be an incorporator; some states insist on natural persons. Usually, one incorporator is sufficient but Arizona and Mississippi require two, and the District of Columbia, North Dakota, Ohio, and Utah demand three.
- Drafting subscription agreements for sale of stock.
- Reserving corporate name (preferably with alternate names).
- Drafting Articles of Incorporation—depending on state practice, it may be either possible or necessary to designate the initial Board of Directors in the Articles of Incorporation.
- Collecting consideration for shares. State law may require that a certain (very minimal) amount of capital, for example, $300 to $1,000—be paid in before corporate operations begin.
- Getting stock certificates, etc. printed (may be contained in corporate kit). Be sure that any transfer restrictions appear on the certificate. State law may require that the shares of a close corporation be identified as such.
- Having corporate seal made up, if needed.
- Filing Articles of Incorporation with appropriate official (usually the Secretary of State).
- Receiving Certificate of Incorporation.
- Ordering corporate kit.

- Arranging for registered agent for service of process and registered office in home state and in any foreign states.
- Holding organization meetings. Depending on state law and, to a limited extent, on the decision of the business founders, the organization meeting may have to be called by the incorporators, initial directors, or stockholders, and may have to be attended by any of those groups—check state law. Be sure that minutes are taken and preserved as required by law. If the initial directors named in the Articles of Incorporation were "straw men," this is the time to elect the actual directors. If any pre-incorporation transactions took place, they should be ratified by the elected Board of Directors.
- Adopting initial bylaws. Again, depending on state law, the power to adopt bylaws may be given to the incorporators, initial directors, or shareholders; the power to amend or repeal bylaws may rest in the Board of Directors, in the shareholders, or as provided by the Articles of Incorporation.
- Issuing share certificates for the stock sold.
- Opening bank account: getting checks printed.
- Qualifying to do business as a foreign corporation in any state in which contacts will be sufficient to require this.
- Filing the Sub S election, if desired.
- Getting EIN (Employer Identification Number).
- Getting sales tax number.
- Making arrangements for deposit of withheld and employer-paid taxes.
- Getting any business licenses required.
- Getting tax forms for any state and local taxes, for example, unincorporated business tax and commercial rent tax.
- Creating a business plan for use in loan and venture capital applications.
- Preparing loan applications.
- Reviewing or drafting promissory notes and security agreements used in raising start-up capital or in financing operations or acquisitions of equipment.
- Drafting buy-sell agreements.
- Purchasing insurance—"key man" and/or insurance used to fund buy-sells, liability, property and casualty, business interruption.

Corporate Powers

Each state provides a "laundry list" of standard corporate powers. This list is not only a means of sparking the drafter's imagination and making him or her think about additional optional powers that can be provided via the Articles of Incorporation or bylaws, but it's a real aid to drafting because the statutory powers need not be specified in the Articles of Incorporation. The following list of statutory corporate powers comes from the revised Model Business Corporation Act Section 302:

- to sue and be sued in corporate name
- to maintain and use a corporate seal (Note: although a corporation can issue documents without using a seal, the seal is evidence that the document was validly executed by the corporation on consent of anyone needed to ratify the transaction)
- to adopt bylaws, dealing with corporate management and regulation, not inconsistent with the provisions of the Articles of Incorporation
- to buy, lease, own, and use real and personal property
- to sell, mortgage, lease, etc., the corporation's property
- to buy, sell, and otherwise deal with ownership interests in, or obligations of, other entities
- to make contracts and guarantees and incur liabilities
- to borrow money, issue obligations, and secure obligations via mortgages, pledges, etc.
- to lend money and accept property as security
- to participate in partnerships, joint ventures, and the like
- to do business either within or outside the state of incorporation
- to elect directors, appoint officers, and hire employees and agents; set duties and compensation; lend money or extend credit
- to set up and fund pension and benefit plans
- to make charitable contributions
- to do any other lawful act furthering corporate objectives

The drafter should also check the relevant state statute; states vary slightly in their list of statutory corporate powers.

Drafting the Articles of Incorporation

The purpose of the Articles of Incorporation is to notify the state (and anyone who cares to read the Articles) of the corporation's basic structure and any departures it makes from the standard boilerplate. Most of the states include a statutory outline of the provisions to be included in the Articles of Incorporation. The list that follows, from the Model Act Section 2.02, is typical:

- the corporate name—which must not be deceptive (for example, indicating that the company is a bank or insurance company, when it is not)—must not be so similar to a name already in use as to be deceptive, and must include "Inc." or a similar indication of corporate status
- the number and type of authorized shares (e.g., total number of shares of all classes; number of shares with par value; number of no-par shares; price of par and no-par shares)

- names and addresses of incorporators
- name of initial registered agent for service of process
- names and addresses of initial directors
- any provision complying with law dealing with corporate purposes, governance, par value, and the like
- any provision that could also be included in the bylaws

Note: many state laws require the Articles of Incorporation to include a statement of corporate purpose—either something along the lines of "to perfect and manufacture the perpetual-motion machine invented by Walter Goodhue," or a general statement such as "for all lawful commercial objectives that may be carried out in corporate form." A requirement that the duration of the corporation—either for a specified number of years or perpetual—be spelled out, is also common.

The Model Act includes a number of optional provisions that may be chosen by a corporation; if so, they must be included in the Articles of Incorporation. They are:

- restrictions on the powers of the Board of Directors, or elimination of the Board of Directors in favor of direct shareholder management
- limitations on directors' compensation
- cumulative voting
- preemptive rights
- requirement of more than a plurality to elect directors
- requirement that certain classes of stock elect certain directors
- restrictions on the power to remove directors
- "staggering" the Board of Directors—that is, arranging for election of only part of the Board in a given year
- requirement that the shareholders have the power to fill vacancies on the Board of Directors
- indemnification of directors, officers, employees may be made more limited than state law provides
- quorum for stockholder meetings can be increased or reduced
- "supermajority"—a requirement that more than a majority of shareholders approve certain actions—can be imposed
- shares can be divided into classes and/or series, perhaps with more than one vote per share for certain classes
- distributions and dividends can be restricted
- redemption of shares—perhaps with reissue of redeemed shares prohibited

Lawyers with access to all fifty state codes should take a look at the pocket part to the Iowa Code. It contains "approved suggested forms," including Articles of Incorporation and bylaws, that should be of interest to a drafter in other states.

Under the Model Act, corporations may also adopt a number of provisions either in the Articles of Incorporation or in the bylaws. For example:

- changes in the number of directors
- prescribed qualifications for directors
- notice requirements for regular or special meetings of the Board of Directors
- limitations on actions by the Board of Directors without meetings (many state statutes allow the directors to act without holding a formal meeting, if they all agree on an action; some states allow "meetings" to take place via telephone conference calls)
- super-majority requirements for Board of Directors meetings
- reductions of quorum for Board meetings (but not below one-third)
- restrictions on participation in meetings by directors who are not physically present (e.g., telephone calls and written statements)
- creation of committees within the Board of Directors
- limitations on the Board of Directors' power to amend bylaws
- issue of shares without share certificates
- transfer restrictions

Qualification of the Foreign Corporation

Although at one time the corporation law of "liberal" states such as Delaware and New Jersey was more permissive than the norm, today the distinctions between state corporation codes are much smaller. (This is not to say that the lawyer who advises start-up businesses doesn't have to be aware of minor state-to-state variations.) Therefore, there are few situations in which it is worthwhile for a business to incorporate in any jurisdication other than the one in which its main operations will be located. These situations might include variations in state taxation (a heavy franchise and/or income tax burden in what would normally be the "home" state; high property taxes on corporate property; high sales taxes) and state law variations in permissible merger and acquisition practice, indemnification of officers and directors, etc.

A corporation that does business in several states will have to qualify as a foreign corporation in the states other than the state of initial incorporation. The concept of "doing business" is a subtle one. A corporation may be "doing business" in a state outside the original state of incorporation for some purposes, but not for others.

The corporation's status and need for registration varies, depending on if the issue is whether a corporation may be sued under a state's long-arm statute (the answer is probably yes, as long as the corporation's products or services allegedly cause some harm in-state, even if the corporation's contacts with the state are minimal), whether the corporation is required to collect and remit state sales taxes on sales made within the state (probably, unless the sale is a pure mail-order sale, procured by sending a catalog through the mail or nationwide advertising, rather than by activities of sales personnel within the state), whether the corporation must qualify as a foreign corporation (probably, unless there are no offices; sales personnel, property, or other indicia of a connection between the business and the foreign state), and whether the state is entitled to tax part of the corporation's income or assets. A basic principle of federalism is that states can tax intrastate activities within their own jurisdiction, but cannot tax purely interstate activities. As the Interstate Income Law, 15 USC Section 381 expresses it 'a state is not permitted to tax income earned within the state by a business whose only activity in the state is solicitation of orders sent outside the forum and filled by shipment outside the forum.'

The process of qualifying as a foreign corporation is a simple one, and the consequences of failure can be dire: the corporation may be denied access to the state's courts to enforce its contracts—but failure to qualify won't prevent the corporation from being sued in the state's courts. Furthermore, the corporation may be fined; an injunction against further business activity may be issued; and the corporation's officers or directors may be held personally liable for the violation.

PRACTICE TIP: *In general, if the corporation will have a continuous course of conduct involving a second, third, etc., state, it should qualify in those states.* [On the interrelation between long-arm statutes and "foreign corporation" qualification statutes *see Eli Lilly & Co. v. Save-on Drugs, Inc.,* 366 US 276 (1961); *Oliver Promotions v. Tams-Witmark Music Library,* 535 F.Supp. 1244 (SDNY 1982); *Lavoie v. General Aerospace Materials Co. Inc.,* (Mass. 2/14/84) CCH Corp. Law Guide Para. 11,914; *Splaine v. Modern Electroplating, Inc.,* (Mass. App. 3/13/84), CCH Corp. Law Guide Para. 11,994; *Lord & Burnham Corp. v. Four Seasons Solar Prods. Corp.,* (Del. Chancery 8/24/84) CCH Corp. Law Guide Para. 11,839; *Rees v. Mosaic Technologies, Inc.* (3d Cir. 8/29/84) 53 LW 2135.]

However, it is well defined that certain isolated acts do not constitute "doing business" and requiring registration. For example:

- maintaining or defending a suit in the state's courts; or settling a case
- holding a shareholder's meeting
- maintaining a bank account
- soliciting orders that must be accepted *outside* the state for a binding contract to be formed
- maintaining an office concerned with securities transfer rather than the transaction of business.

As an example, consider *Pacamor Bearings, Inc. v. Molon Motors & Coil Inc.,* CCH Corp. Law Guide ¶11,856 (N.Y. Sup. 1984): an Illinois corporation sending merchandise by mail to a New York buyer, but not qualified as a foreign corporation in New York, and lacking any office, property, telephone, or bank account within New York, was not "doing business" in New York, and could not be sued in New York.

To qualify, the corporation must pay a small fee and must not use a name that is deceptive or deceptively similar to the name used or reserved by a domestic corporation. Most of the states allow foreign corporations to "register" names in a process very similar to the reservation of a name by a domestic corporation; cf. Tenn. Op. AG #84-089, 3/15/84, precluding adoption of a name misleadingly similar to a name already in use within the state, so as to risk misleading or deceiving the public, with *Trans-America Airlines, Inc. v. Kenton,* CCH Corp. Law Guide ¶11,809, (Delaware Sup. 1985), permitting registration of a potentially confusingly similar name, as long as the names can be distinguished by the Secretary of State.

Depending on state practice, it may be necessary to submit a certified copy of the original Articles of Incorporation or Certificate of Incorporation issued by the state authorities, to submit a certificate of good standing from the corporate authorities of the home state, and to submit information such as:

- the corporation's name
- the state of original incorporation
- the date of incorporation
- the stated duration (e.g., five years; perpetual)
- the address of corporation's principal office
- the address of the corporation's proposed registered office in the state in which qualification is sought
- the name and address of proposed registered agent
- the names and addresses of the corporation's directors and officers
- the corporation's authorized capitalization, analyzed by class and series, and allocating between par and no-par shares
- a similar breakdown of issued shares
- the corporation's stated capital in dollars
- the estimated value of the property the corporation will own in the next year; the estimated overall volume of business and the volume of business projected to be done in the state in which qualification is sought.

Allocation of potentially taxable income among states is predominantly a problem of the going corporation, so it will merely be touched on here. However, the business's founders should be aware of the possibility of income taxation by several states and should be prepared to make the appropriate tax returns and payments.

The classic statement comes from *Northwestern States Portland Cement Co. v. Minnesota,* 358 US 450 (1959): "The entire net income of a corporation, generated by interstate as well as intrastate activities, may be fairly apportioned among the states for tax purposes by formulas utilizing in-state aspects of interstate affairs."

Due process requires a minimal connection between the interstate activities and the taxing state, and also requires a rational relationship between the income attributed to the state and the portion of assets within the state and business carried on in the state.

These principles have been upheld by many later cases, e.g, *Mobil Oil Corp. v. Comm'r of Taxes of Vermont* 445 U.S. 425 (1980), *Armco Inc. v. Hardesty,* 467 U.S. 638 (1984), and *Bank Building and Equipment Corp. of America v. Dir. of Revenue,* CCH Corp. Law Guide ¶11,855 (Mo. Sup. 1985). However, states must not discriminate between in-state and out-of-state businesses, or between manufacturing and wholesaling activities. Review has been granted in two Washington cases dealing with that state's wholesale business and business and occupation taxes: #85-1963, *Tyler Pipe Industries, Inc. v. Wash. State. Dep't of Revenue* (105 Wash.2d 318, 715 P.2d 123,1986) and #85-2006, *National Can Corp. v. Wash. State Dep't of Revenue* (105 Wash.2d 327, 715 P.2d 128, 1986). The Supreme Court may dramatically limit state powers in this area.

Bylaws

In general, bylaws can include anything related to corporate purposes, powers, and governance that is not illegal and that is not required to be stated in the Articles of Incorporation. The difference is that, in general, it is a lot easier to amend or repeal a bylaw than to change the Articles of Incorporation because the Articles are a public document and an elaborate statutory procedure is required. Although the bylaws are not permitted to violate state law or to contradict the Articles of Incorporation, they otherwise have a great deal of latitude. They can deal with many aspects of the corporation's external business and internal governance and are binding on the corporation, its stockholders, and on third parties who have notice of the bylaws. Issues typically addressed in the bylaws include:

- the location of the corporation's offices
- the annual meetings of stockholders and directors—where and when they will be held, how notice will be given, the record date (date for determining whether the buyer or seller of stock is the owner of record entitled to vote), quorum, and agenda
- when and why special meetings can be held, on whose call, and on what terms
- the composition of the Board of Directors, whether a large board will be elected in "staggered" fashion, their term of office, how they can be removed, how successor directors will be chosen, how much they will be compensated for service as directors, circumstances under which the corporation will indemnify them
- what officers the corporation will have (state law often requires a president, vice-president, secretary, and treasurer, and permits other officers if desired), qualifications required of officers, their terms of office and duties,

their compensation, how they can be removed and replaced, and terms of indemnification

- what the corporation's fiscal year will be
- policy on dividends and corporate reserves
- the shareholder's right to inspect the corporate books and records. Most state statutes provide a minimum right which cannot be abridged; if the minority shareholders are powerful (or if they vote together), they may be able to supplement the statutory rights with broader access to records, which in turn will be helpful in case of dispute or possible squeeze-out.
- corporate policy on transactions in which directors are interested parties— for example, buying supplies from another corporation owned or controlled by a director
- how the bylaws may be amended

EXAMPLE: The projected capitalization of Geneva Confections, Inc. includes a large loan, a second mortgage on one of the founder's homes, and purchase of stock by 15 individuals. The stockholders will be investing amounts ranging from $5,000 to $75,000; five of the stockholders will be employed by the corporation, two of them on a part-time basis. The largest single holding is 22%, followed by 14% and 10% (these are the three full-time employees). The remaining 54% is shared more or less equally among the other 12 stockholders. The minority stockholders have enough negotiating power to make sure that the corporation's bylaws contain restrictions on the salaries of shareholder-employees, cumulative voting, expansive rights to inspect books and records, and a policy that the corporation limit its retention of earnings in favor of paying dividends. These provisions make it harder (although not impossible) for the full-time employees to run the corporation exclusively for their own benefit and to the detriment of the minority shareholders.

The Organization Meeting

Once the corporation has been structured and the Articles of Incorporation drafted and filed, the corporation must hold an initial organization meeting. Depending on state law variations, the meeting may have to be called by a majority of the incorporators or a majority of the initial Board of Directors named in the Articles of Incorporation. The normal attendees are the initial directors, but some state statutes specify a meeting of incorporators or stockholders.

The task of the meeting is to begin the corporation's formal existence:

- to file the evidence of incorporation (the second executed copy of the Articles of Incorporation; the Certificate of Incorporation issued by the state authorities) usually by inserting them into the minute book furnished as part of the corporate kit
- adoption of the bylaws (unless state law calls for adoption of bylaws by a different body)

- adoption of a corporate seal
- resignation of the initial directors, election of a Board of Directors to serve until the first annual meeting—in the start-up context, usually the same people
- ratification of pre-incorporation transactions
- if the corporation is a close one and stockholder agreements have been entered into (see page 85), adoption of the agreements by the corporation
- election of officers
- adoption of a form of stock certificate—again, usually already provided in the corporate kit
- adoption of resolutions dealing with the issuance and consideration for stock—most states have laws providing that shares may be issued for cash, noncash property, and past services—but not for notes or future services. Many states make it explicit that share consideration can be used to defray reasonable organizational expenses without impairing the shares' status as "fully paid and non-assessable." (See page 51 for a discussion of the tax status of start-up expenses.)
- adoption of resolution authorizing Sub S election, if desired
- designation of corporation's principal office
- adoption of resolution opening bank account(s) in designated bank(s). The bank may demand that the resolution take a certain form, so check with the bank before the meeting.

The organization meeting, like all corporate meetings, must be evidenced by minutes in proper form. (If a corporate kit is used, there will be minute forms included.) The minutes must indicate the meeting's date, time, place and purpose; must show that a quorum was present; must summarize the issues considered, including those on which no action was taken; and must include the text of any corporate resolutions adopted. State law sets the requirements for signing the minutes—usually the Secretary must sign, but further signatures may be required. All participants should be sent a copy of the minutes because all meetings begin with approval of the minutes of the prior meeting.

PRACTICE TIP: Where should the minute book be kept? Many corporations (and lawyers) find it more convenient for the lawyer to have custody of the minute book and the stock ledger so that he or she can refer to them as necessary and update them as required. But check state law—it may require that these documents be kept at the corporation's registered office. (No problem, of course, if the attorney's office is designated as the registered office.)

Incorporation of a Going Business

In general, incorporating an existing proprietorship or partnership is quite similar to incorporating a start-up business. However, certain issues exist in the incorporation of a going business that need not be considered in a start-up: for example, the rights of creditors of the predecessor business and what will become of the predecessor business's pension plan.

The attorney seldom need worry about tax problems. Section 351 provides a mechanism for tax-free incorporation. Under Section 358, a sole proprietor's basis for stock and securities issued by the new corporation equals the basis of assets transferred, and no gain or loss is recognized on the transfer (Section 351). Rev.Rul. 85-164, 1985-42 IRB 6 raises an interesting issue, and disposes of it by indicating that a proprietor can not "match up" property transferred with particular shares of stock in the new corporation: the aggregate basis of all properties transferred is allocated among all the stock and securities received, in proportion to fair market value.

One of the attorney's tasks is to make sure that all appropriate assets really are transferred to the corporation—incorporation does not automatically transfer title to assets. If a partnership is incorporated, consent of all partners must be obtained. No one can be forced to become a stockholder against his will and no partnership can be bound, outside the normal course of its business, without consent of all partners.

The new corporation will be responsible for the predecessor business's debts if it expressly assumes them, if an agreement to assume can be implied (e.g., if the corporation continues to use the telephone lines connected for—and billed to—the predecessor partnership), or if the corporation is a participant in a fraudulent transfer. *Maddux & Sons Inc. v. Local 395 Health & Welfare Trust Fund*, 125 Ariz. 475, 610 P2d 477 (1980) says that a corporation taking over as alter ego of a proprietorship is bound by the proprietorship's union contract, to the extent that the corporation's activities come within the terms of the agreement.

At the other end of the scale, former proprietors and partners may find themselves still personally liable despite the incorporation—if the new corporation's creditors have not been notified of the changed status [*Kapp v. Naturelle*, 611 F2d 703 (8th Cir. 1979)]. So part of the attorney's task is to make sure the business's creditors do get this notice and to instruct the clients to avoid the free-and-easy accounting practices that too often characterize noncorporate businesses. (See pages 65–68 for a discussion of piercing the corporate veil, which is often triggered by commingling of personal and business finances.)

Under Rev.Rul. 71-541, 1971-2 CB 209, the assets of a Keogh plan can be transferred to a qualified plan post-incorporation. There will be no tax consequences so long as the participants do not have an unrestricted right to receive the plan assets as a result of the change over. The transferred assets continue to be governed by the Keogh plan rules, not the qualified plan rules.

PRACTICE TIP: *Incorporation of a going business will require the opening of new bank accounts and, perhaps, a review of who should have authority to sign checks. A partnership's buy-sell agreement must be redrafted with the corporate status in mind. New stationery should be printed. The change in status certainly requires a review of accounting practices; this may be a good time to streamline the practices or to shift from manual to computerized accounting.*

3

RAISING START-UP FUNDS

One of the most important challenges facing the new business is how it will get the funds it needs to prepare for business, start operations, and keep going until enough business has been generated to make the new enterprise a profitable one.

For sole proprietors the problems are intellectually simple, though the practical difficulties can be far greater or even insuperable. The proprietor invests as much of his or her own money as is possible or as he or she deems prudent, and can also borrow to support the new enterprise provided, of course, that his or her personal credit is good enough to attract lenders.

Partnerships can borrow money and, of course, all the partners will be jointly and severally liable for the partnership's debts; a fact which is encouraging to potential creditors but can be discouraging to potential partners. One of the most important functions of a well-drafted partnership agreement is to specify the conditions under which partners will be expected to supply additional capital, how the contribution will affect their share of partnership assets and liabilities, and what will happen if they can't or won't supply the capital.

Under Code Section 721, the general rule is that neither a partner nor the partnership will recognize gain or loss on contribution of property in return for a partnership interest. Section 722 defines the basis of such a partnership interest as the amount of money contributed plus the adjusted basis of any fair market value transferred.

A corporation has the option of borrowing and the theoretical attribute of limited liability, so that the stockholders will not be liable for the debt. However, the attribute is theoretical because a lender would be foolish to lend to a start-up corporation that has no track record, no receivables, and precious few assets. In the real world, the lender will probably require personal guarantees from at least one shareholder.

A corporation also has another option for raising funds: the sale of its stock. Initial public offerings of stock are beyond the scope of this book. As for the more common situation in which a business commences operation as a private corporation, care must be taken to make sure that the stock is not offered to the "public," as defined by securities laws, in a way that triggers the obligation to register the stock. (The federal exemptions from registration are discussed later in this chapter.) Practitioners should be aware that, just because an issue of stock is not subject to federal registration, does not automatically mean an exemption from state "Blue Sky" regulation—it is not unlikely that state registration, albeit probably in summary form, will be required.

Corporate Borrowing

It can be very difficult, even with personal guarantees, for a start-up business to get bank loans. After all, the banks have plenty of applicants—many of them well-established businesses—for loans. In addition to outright secured or unsecured term loans in a particular amount, banks may offer informal credit lines, permitting borrowing of a certain amount per quarter. These credit lines are usually used to buy inventory; the expectation is that repayment will be made as soon as the inventory is sold.

Many businesses also have revolving credit arrangements which permit them to borrow up to a certain limit. These arrangements frequently carry a commitment fee in addition to the interest rate.

Although start-up corporations have little negotiating power, and it is unlikely that the attorney can get a bank to change the loan terms, at least the attorney can inform the clients of the terms and make sure that they are prepared to comply with them. For example, loan agreements frequently specify that the death or insolvency of any guarantor constitutes default—so the business can find itself in default because Uncle Irving has died, even if loan payments continue to be made on schedule and in the proper amounts.

Business loans frequently require a "compensating balance"—that a certain amount be kept in the business's bank account with the lending institution—so that the effective amount borrowed is reduced. Sometimes "relationship banking"—maintenance of several accounts with the same institution (e.g., a business checking account, deposit accounts for withheld taxes, personal accounts of corporate officers)—will result in a slightly lower interest rate on corporate borrowing. However, if the loan agreement contains a "setoff" provision, the bank will be able to deduct overdue loan payments from the business's and guarantors' accounts with the bank. Setoff provisions are frequently drafted to permit setoff without notice, with the possibility of bouncing checks and a spiralling loss of confidence in the corporation among other creditors.

Businesses frequently acquire equipment on a conditional sale or secured loan basis creating a very real possibility that various sellers and lenders (for example, a bank extending a secured term loan; the seller of the business's machinery) will have security interests in the same collateral. One of the lawyer's jobs is to straighten all this out. It is common for banks contemplating loans to businesses to require that the business's other creditors execute subordination agreements, guaranteeing that their interests will be subordinate to the bank's if the business fails. Preparing and securing these agreements is another task for the attorney.

Yet another task: educating clients about the provisions of the various loan and security agreements, and about the clients' rights as borrowers. Business loans are *not* covered by the Truth in Lending Act (15 USC Section 1601) even if the borrowers lack business sophistication; even if part of the proceeds will be used for personal expenses of business owners [*Winkle v. Grand National Bank*, 601 SW2d 559 (Ark. 1980)], and even if the loan used for business purposes is secured by a mortgage on the personal residence of a business owner [*Poe v. First National Bank*, 597 F2d 895 (5th Cir. 1979); *Weingarten v. First Mortgage Corporation*, 466 F. Supp. 349 (ED Pa. 1979)].

PRACTICE TIP: *It will probably be necessary for the corporation's attorney and accountant to work together to prepare loan applications.* A typical loan application calls for extensive financial disclosure and preparation of a business plan. Information requested might include:

- the amount and length of loan requested
- collateral offered
- guarantees offered
- purpose of the loan, for example, whether the money will be used as operating capital or to purchase equipment or inventory
- proposed repayment terms
- the corporation's history, type of business or business plans, résumés of directors, officers, and major stockholders
- existing capital and its sources

- number and compensation of employees
- pension and benefit plans, if any
- any tax returns already filed
- income statements or projected income statements for the period after the business starts operations
- balance sheets or projected balance sheets
- projections of the effect the money sought to be borrowed will have on corporate operations
- a three-year cash flow projection

If the loan is approved, the loan terms will probably call for continuing financial controls, and the corporation will probably have to submit financial statements at intervals and submit to grilling if the actual results don't match the projections.

Venture Capital

If your client contemplates a high-tech business (e.g., has a patented or patentable invention at or near the production stage), it may be possible to attract the attention of a venture capitalist or venture capital firm. (Note: accepting venture capital is almost certain to terminate a Sub S election either because the money comes from a corporation—an unacceptable Sub S stockholder—or because part of the venture capitalist's interest is in the form of preferred stock, which violates the "one-class-of-stock" requirement.)

Venture capitalists usually seek a Return on Investment Reward Percentage (appreciation in assets and annual revenue derived from the venture capitalist's investment, divided by the investment itself) of 50% or more for start-up companies; 40% to 50% from companies that have a product in production and have shipped some orders, 35% to 40% from operating companies that have not yet become profitable, and 25% to 30% from profitable companies seeking expansion capital. Venture capitalists also tend to prefer a quick turnaround: 3 to 5 years' participation, then exiting gracefully with a pocketful of profit (at least five times the original investment).

To attract venture capital, the start-up business must have a very attractive business plan; a strong management team with a good track record—and who have invested a convincing amount of their own money in the venture; and credible projections of 25% annual growth in sales and pre-tax profit, and of at least 30% annual return on the venture capitalist's investment. Therefore, the attorney and accountant for the new business must work together to prepare believable projections of sales, expenses, and cash flow. A venture capital proposal must also disclose the initial capital sought, and estimated later capital needs; how the product or service will be marketed; what makes it unique; if it is appropriate for subcontracting; the expected sales volume that can be reached; the corporation's existing capital and management team; and its existing liabilities.

EXAMPLE: The Roffman-Martin-O'Toole team (discussed earlier), eventually incorporated as Executive Perks, Inc., might be a prime candidate for venture capital if the new coffee-making method is not only patentable but offers advantages to coffee drinkers that are substantial enough to overcome their loyalty to existing methods of coffee brewing. The potential market of coffee drinkers is very large and patent protection ensures that there will be no direct competition during the term of the patent. (However, it may be possible for others to adapt the patented technology in a way that is itself patentable—and this is a real risk if the new product becomes successful.)

There will be some problems with venture capital, though. A part-time Chief Financial Officer (CFO) might not be considered adequate, and O'Toole might have to be demoted or dismissed and replaced with an experienced, full-time CFO. That could be expensive for the corporation—she has an employment contract. As discussed above, venture capital would probably terminate the Sub S election; the three stockholders must take this into account in evaluating possible venture capital deals.

One of the important points to watch out for is that the venture capitalist doesn't get too high a percentage of the corporation's voting and nonvoting stock in return for a comparatively small investment. The effect of transferring a large block of stock to the venture capitalist on the corporation's balance of power must also be considered.

The outcome of successful venture capital negotiations is an agreement between the venture capitalist and the financed company. Typically, the venture capital agreement is a very long document specifying the amount and timing of financing to be supplied by the venture capitalist, the allocation between straight debt and securities to be issued to the venture capitalist, the financed company's positive covenants (agreeing to do things such as paying all liabilities on time, maintaining key-man insurance on top employees, continued compliance with all applicable laws), negative covenants (e.g., "anti-dilution" provisions that protect the venture capitalist against loss of value due to issuance of a great deal of new stock), and representations and warranties (e.g., that signing the venture capital agreement is not a violation of other agreements such as bank loan documents and audited financial statements).

Securities Law

It is clear that, if stock is available to all and sundry, the offering of stock is a public offering and cannot be made legally without going to the trouble and expense of registration under the 1933 Securities Act. It is equally clear that a sole stockholder can issue all of a corporation's stock to himself without furnishing himself with disclosure materials. In between, private issue exemptions are available if the federal rules are complied with. The factors involved in the exemption are seldom hard and fast; there's no "litmus test" distinguishing between public and private offerings. The distinction is one of fact and depends on the amount of disclosure offered and the degree to which investors require protection—which, in turn, depends on their resources and financial sophistication [*Mary S. Krech Trust v. Lake Apartments*, 642 F2d 98 (5th Cir. 1981)].

Although Rule 10b-5, forbidding fraud and material misrepresentation, applies to private as well as public issues of stock, exemptions from the need to register the offering are available for small issues; for issues that are entirely intrastate; and for issues that are considered nonpublic because there are few offerees and/or all the offerees are sophisticated. In short, registration exemptions are available whenever it is deemed unnecessary for the federal government to intervene to protect potential stockholders from inadequate disclosure.

The classic case is *SEC v. Ralston Purina Co.*, 346 US 119 (1953), which holds that the private offering exemption under Securities Act Section 4(2) is limited to offerings made only to people "able to fend for themselves," who do not require the protection offered by registration because of their own investment sophistication or because the issuer has provided them with the same amount and type of information they would have gotten via registration. To a certain extent, there's a trade-off; an unregistered issue may be permissible with less disclosure if the offerees are more sophisticated, or with less sophistication if more disclosure is provided.

Securities Act Section 3(b) allows the SEC to promulgate rules and regulations exempting issues with an aggregate price of $5 million or less from the registration requirements—but only if the public interest does not require registration, given the small amount of stock involved, or the limited nature of any public offering involved. Section 4(2) of the Act exempts transactions that do not involve a public offering.

Section 4(6) permits sales of up to $5 million in stock without registration if all buyers are "accredited investors," there is no public advertising or solicitation, and Form D is filed with the SEC to indicate reliance on the exemption. (An accredited investor is "any person who, on the basis of such factors as financial sophistication, net worth, knowledge, and experience in financial matters, or amount of assets under management qualifies as an accredited investor under rules the Commission shall prescribe"—a category comprising pension funds, banks, registered investment companies, and the wealthy and well-advised.)

A basic premise of the exemptions from registration (other than Regulation A offerings, discussed on page 45) is that the buyers of the stock buy it for investment, not speculation (this qualification is not required of institutional investors).

PRACTICE TIP: *It is good practice for the issuer to sell the stock subject to an "investment letter" expressing the buyer's understanding that the stock is to be held for at least two years before transfer. It is equally good practice for the seller of an intrastate offering to get a similar letter from the buyers, expressing their commitment not to sell to an out-of-state buyer for at least nine months after the issuer's last intrastate sale of the issue.* The certificates should probably carry a legend that the stock is not registered and is purchased for investment, not speculation; and it is probably good policy to instruct the corporation's transfer agent not to transfer the stock in violation of the restrictions. The corporation's attorney should check state law—depending on the state, the transfer restrictions may be a mandatory condition of "Blue Sky-ing" the issue.

Rule 147: Exemption from registration is available for purely intrastate offerings under Rule 147 [explicating Securities Act Section 3(a)(11)]. There is no limit on the amount of stock that can be offered under Rule 147 provided that all buyers and all offerees are residents of the state in which the issuing corporation is incorporated and has its principal place of business. The test for offerees is whether they have their principal residence within the state.

To qualify, the issuer must derive at least 80% of its gross revenues for the year and 80% of its assets from activities and real estate within the state. There is a further limitation: 80% of the proceeds of the offering must be used in-state.

See, for instance, *SEC v. McDonald Investment Co.*, 343 F. Supp. 343 (D.Minn. 1972)—loans secured by property outside the state impair the availability of the exemption by preventing the issuer from meeting the 80% "doing business" requirement, even though the corporation's only office was in Minnesota and all offerees were Minnesota residents. It is permissible to use the proceeds of the offering to buy wine outside the state in question, for resale within the state: *Adventures in Wine*, CCH Securities Law Reporter ¶80,952 (1976-77 Transfer Binder).

Regulation A: This is the "small offering" exemption. The maximum offering is $1.5 million. Furthermore, "affiliates" are not permitted to offer more than $100,000 of their stock as part of the Regulation A offering—so this exemption can't be used as a "get rich quick" device for the corporation's original stockholders. (An "affiliate" is a person with the potential to control the corporation—for example, a top executive; however, this limitation is not applied to estates of affiliates.)

Most United States and Canadian corporations can use Regulation A. The exceptions are registered investment companies; companies selling fractional undivided interests in oil, gas, or mineral rights; and companies that have already been in trouble with the SEC, or whose officers, directors, or general partners have already fallen afoul of the "bad boy" rules. It is unlikely that a start-up company would have had time to anger the SEC. It is possible that corporate management will contain a person who has already had a brush with the SEC; however, application of the "bad boy" rules can be waived by the SEC in the interests of justice.

To qualify for Regulation A, the issuer must make extensive disclosures, using the SEC's Notification Form 1-A at least ten business days before the initial offering—and make an offering circular available to potential buyers at least 48 hours before the sale confirmation is mailed—a "mini-registration" process which is, however, faster and cheaper than the full-scale registration process.

In deciding whether the issue falls within the $1.5 million limit, the issuer must "integrate" the offering. In this context, this means that all stock, which is really part of a single transaction, must be included within the $1.5 million limit. For start-up companies and companies that did not have net income from operations in one or both of the two years preceding the Regulation A offering, all these securities must be included in calculating the $1.5 million:

- stock issued at any time with noncash assets or services as consideration

- stock issued to the corporation's officers and directors
- stock issued to underwriters, dealers, and security salespersons involved in floating the Regulation A issue itself

These limitations might make Regulation A unattractive if the corporation needs a great deal of capital, and if much stock has already been issued to the corporation's founders, officers, and directors or to those involved in floating the issue. The SEC will, however, suspend application of the integration rules if stock otherwise subject to integration is placed in escrow and not offered to the public within one year of the Regulation A offering. This may be a feasible option for your clients. If not, consider a Regulation D offering or, if a moderate amount of capital is required, the expedited registration process (using Form S-18) for certain offerings under $7.5 million.

Regulation A offerings are allowed to use "tombstone" ads or radio or television advertisements that are comparably restrained in tone—for example, simply state the name of the issuer, the title of the security, and where to get the offering circular (SEC Rule 255).

Regulation D: Of course, all corporations must comply with the federal securities laws. However, to simplify the task of compliance, the SEC has issued a number of "safe harbor" rules. If a corporation follows the safe harbor rules, it is automatically in compliance—and it may be in compliance with the law if it fits within the terms of the statute, even if it doesn't fit within the safe harbor rules.

Regulation D provides three safe harbor rules, slightly different in the terms under which exemption from registration will be available. But remember, it is still possible for the issuer to sell stock legally by complying with the terms of the Securities Act even if none of the "safe harbors" are used.

Rule 504 permits a limited offering and sale of up to $500,000 within a 12-month period. Notice of sale must be filed with the SEC. There may not be any general advertising or solicitation (unless the offering is registered in a state that requires a disclosure document) but there is no limit on the number of buyers, and no particular qualifications are required of investors. Most companies are permitted to use Rule 504—the exceptions are investment companies and companies required to report under the 1934 Securities Exchange Act. Resale of the stock by buyers is restricted—again, unless the state requires a disclosure document.

The $500,000 limit is computed by including sales in the past 12 months under this rule, Rule 505, or Regulation A—and including all sales that were made in violation of the registration requirements.

These days, half a million isn't much; it may be far less than your client needs to start up. In that case, a Rule 505 offering (offers and sales up to $5 million within a 12-month period) may be preferable.

Rule 505 offerings must be made without general advertising or solicitation. The offering can be made to any number of accredited investors, and not to more than 35 nonaccredited investors. The test is whether the issuer reasonably believes that the alleged accredited investors fall into this group. Therefore, it is good practice to include a representation of accreditation in the "investment letter" provided by buyers. A notice of sale must be filed with the SEC. The $5 million limit included Rule 505 sales, Regulation A sales, and violative sales as well as Rule 505 sales within the 12-month period.

Rule 506 permits offerings and sales in any amount, provided that there is no general advertising or solicitation, and provided that there are not more than 35 unaccredited investors involved as buyers. The number of purchasers for Rule 506 purposes does not include a purchaser's spouse or a relative or spouse of a relative living in the same household as an investor, nor does it include trusts and corporations controlled by an investor. (There's no limit on sales to accredited investors.) All buyers must be "sophisticated" investors. Accredited investors are always considered sophisticated; a private individual can qualify as sophisticated based on income and investment experience, or if he or she has a "purchaser representative."

The definition of "accredited investor" applies to:

- a natural person whose individual net worth is greater than $1 million or who has had an income of $200,000 or more in the past two years, with a reasonable expectation of matching that income level in the year of the purchase
- a natural person who buys $150,000 or more of the stock under offer for any combination of cash, forgiveness of debt, marketable securities, or an unconditional promise to pay within five years. However, this rule is only applicable if the purchase represents 20% or less of the net worth of the purchaser and his or her spouse.

The net worth of the purchaser's spouse and the value of their principal residence can be counted toward the net worth limitations, but the income of the purchaser's spouse and unrealized gains on securities may not be counted. Under SEC Staff Interpretations, a combination of $75,000 cash and a $75,000 letter of credit does not equal $150,000 worth of stock—a personal note for the entire amount would probably have qualified.

How can the issuer attract the attention of would-be purchasers if general solicitation is forbidden and even "tombstone" type advertisements are unavailable? Seminars and meetings are permitted as long as general advertisement or solicitation of the seminar is avoided. However, advertisements in trade journals and publication of a newsletter sent to accredited investors have been held to violate the prohibition on advertising.

Under both Rules 505 and 506, if there are any unaccredited investors involved, all offerees must receive the prescribed disclosures. And for all three Regulation D rules, the issuer must file five copies of the SEC's Form D with the Washington SEC office (*not* the regional office closest to the issuer's place of business) within 15 days after the first sale in the offering. The issuer must refile every 6 months, with a last filing 30 days after the final sale in an offering.

It is worth noting that 22 states (Alabama, Arizona, Colorado, Connecticut, Delaware, Georgia, Hawaii, Idaho, Kentucky, Louisiana, Maine, Maryland, Missouri, Nebraska, New Jersey, North Carolina, Ohio, Oklahoma, Oregon, Utah, Virginia, and Washington) have an exemption similar either to Rule 506 or its predecessor SEC Rule 146.

Blue Sky Laws and Registration Exemptions: Ironically, "Blue Skying" (qualifying under state securities laws) an initial public offering is usually fairly simple because most states permit "registration by coordination," allowing the federal registration documents to serve as state registration documents as well. Some states add a layer of regulation by submitting offerings to "merit review," where the soundness of the underlying issue, as well as the quantity and accuracy of disclosure, is scrutinized.

State Blue Sky Laws typically contain an exemption from registration for sales to institutional investors, though the definition is not necessarily identical to the federal concept of the accredited investor. Most state laws do not set a dollar limit on exempt offerings.

Many states permit an exemption from registration if fewer than ten investors are involved; some states limit this to ten offerees, others to ten purchasers out of a larger number of offerees. The state definition frequently excludes banks, employee pension plans, investment companies, and the like, from the count of ten. It is also typical for pre-incorporation subscription transactions, with fewer than ten subscribers and no pre-incorporation payment for securities or sales commissions, to be exempted from state registration requirements. TIP: Some states deny the exemption if the purchaser representatives get a commission, so consider structuring the deal so that the securities dealers or other purchaser representatives receive a flat fee if the corporation is starting up in one of these states (e.g., California).

To summarize, compliance with the intrastate offering exemption, or an exemption based on the size of the offering or the number or sophistication of offerees and purchasers, can permit a corporation to raise up to $5 million (depending on the exemption). Some disclosure will be required to the buyers and the SEC, but the burden will be much smaller than if registration were required.

EXAMPLE: Gerald Hiroshi is impressed by the success of black-owned companies selling cosmetics and hair-care preparations, and believes that he can achieve similar success with products for people of Oriental heritage. He feels that developing, manufacturing, and launching these products will require start-up capital of approximately $2 million. He has personal assets of $100,000 that he can devote to this task.

He would prefer to start out with a private corporation—first, to avoid the difficulties and expense of regulation; second, to give himself and the other initial stockholders an opportunity to benefit by an Initial Public Offering which he believes will be much more successful if the corporation is already profitable and whose products have attained some publicity.

Hiroshi has many alternatives for raising the remaining $1.9 million; the choice of the optimum alternative depends on both legal and practical matters. For instance, if he has wealthy relatives in several states who are willing to invest and who wish to become stockholders rather than lenders or loan guarantors, he would probably be better off accepting them as investors and foregoing the possibility of a Rule 147 intrastate offering. If he can borrow $400,000 or more, he can raise up to $1.5 million via a Regulation A offering; because no stock has yet been offered, "integration" is not a problem. Of course, Rule 504 is unavailable, because far more than $500,000 is required. Rule 505 is a real possibility, because less than $5 million is required; the only problem might be finding the right mix of accredited investors and not more than 35 non-accredited investors, when general advertising and solicitation is ruled out. Rule 506 is also a possibility, provided that enough "sophisticated" investors can be found without general advertising and solicitation.

4

TAX QUESTIONS ABOUT THE NEW ENTERPRISE

A full treatment of partnership and corporate tax is beyond the scope of this book. However, certain questions are likely to arise in the start-up process: for instance, the tax treatment of start-up expenses; the availability of the home office deduction for very small, home-based businesses; the problem of "thin" incorporation, and the business' compliance burden in terms of tax withholding, estimated tax, and FICA and FUTA tax.

Start-Up Expenses

Without the relief provided by Code §§195 and 248, all the expenses of organizing a business would have to be capitalized—all very well if and when the business is being sold, but not of much help to entrepreneurial clients looking for tax deductions on this year's return. Section 195 permits amortization of qualifying start-up costs over a period of at least 60 months. Or, if the business prefers, the expenses can be capitalized: amortization is optional.

The election to amortize must be made not later than the time for filing the tax return for the year of the start-up; and the election is not available if the business is never, in fact, started up [Code Section 195(b)(1)] or if the business has a determinable useful life of less than 60 months (Senate Report 96-1036, p. 14).

The procedure for making the election is given by Reg. 1.248-1(c). The first year's return must include a statement of election, specifying the number of months (at least 60) over which amortization will take place; the month in which the corporation started doing business (defined by Reg. Section 1.248-1(a)(3) as the time when operating activities start, not merely the time at which the charter has been issued); and dates, descriptions, and amounts of expenditures to be amortized.

Naturally, many clients want everything to be considered an ordinary and necessary expense of a going business (and hence deductible), because a current deduction usually seems more worthwhile than amortization over five years. In theory, of course, the business will be so prosperous five years hence that the amortization deduction will be precious; but that day may never arrive.

Code Section 248(b) gives some guidance as to which expenses are treated as start-up expenses as opposed to operating expenses of a going business. They are:

- incident to the creation of the business
- chargeable to the capital account for accounting purposes
- of a type that *would* be amortizable over the business's limited life, if indeed it had a limited life. For example:
  - legal services such as those involved in drafting a corporation's Articles of Incorporation
  - accounting services such as those rendered in selecting a fiscal year and setting up the business's books
  - fees paid to the state of incorporation
  - expenses of the organization meeting
  - directors' fees paid to the initial, temporary Board of Directors.

The initial fees to the state of incorporation are tricky. If the sums really are *fees*, they must either be amortized or capitalized; but if they're *taxes*, they're deductible in the year paid as ordinary and necessary business expenses. The line between fees and taxes is a fine one. I suggest that you consult the state statute (cites given in the cite table on pages 114–115) and abide by the characterization in the statute. The costs of qualifying as a foreign corporation are deductible—presumably because there must be an existing, operating corporation before qualification is necessary or even possible.

The problems of characterization are especially tricky for businesses involved in real estate development. The IRS is likely to treat activities before development or even before occupancy as start-up expenses rather than as expenses of a going business [*Davis v. Comm'r*, TC Memo 1983-160 and *Johnsen v. Comm'r*, 55 LW2048

(6th Cir. 1986)]. *Davis* involved legal fees for buying land incurred by a partnership whose business purpose was development of the land as trailer parks. The fees were held to be nondeductible capital expenditures because the partnership was construed not to have any trade or business to carry out until it obtained a zoning variance permitting development.

Similarly, the limited partnership involved in *Johnsen* prepared for operation of an apartment project in year 1, but the project was neither completed nor occupied—and no rent deposits were accepted—until year 2. Thus, the limited partnership was not engaged in a trade or business in year 1, so commitment, management, and guarantee fees paid in year 1 were not deductible as ordinary and necessary business expenses. Nor, in the opinion of the Sixth Circuit, were they §212 expenses for production of income.

PRACTICE TIP: These cases highlight the importance of timing. It may be worthwhile to delay a start-up so that preliminary processes can be completed during the business's first taxable year.

Routine Tax Compliance

Apropos of which ... unless the business is organized and operated as a sole proprietorship, it will have certain federal tax reporting, and possibly payment, burdens. (The sole proprietor's quarterly estimated tax returns will reflect the business's profits.)

Partnerships must file annual federal information returns on or before the fifteenth day of the fourth month after the end of the taxable year. The relevant form (Form 1065) includes:

- Schedule A—income, deductions, and cost of goods sold.
- Schedule D—(there isn't any Schedule B or C) partnership capital gains and losses.
- Schedule H—income derived from rentals of partnership property.
- Schedule I—bad debts.
- Schedule K—total income, credits, and deductions available to all the partners, broken down into one Schedule K-1 per partner analyzing individual partners' entitlement to income and deduction items. Allocations of gain are permitted to be disproportionate; in a loss partnership, partners are not entitled to a loss deduction in excess of adjusted basis for the partnership interest or the amount for which the partner is at risk.
- Schedule L—comparison of partnership's opening and closing balance sheets for the taxable year.
- Schedule M—changes in partners' capital accounts.
- Schedule N—identification of partners and relative shares in the partnership.

S corporations must file an annual Form 1120S information return on or before the fifteenth day of the *third* month after the end of the taxable year. The 1120S is similar to the 1065, containing:

- Gross income, deduction, and tax computations.
- Schedule A—cost of goods sold.
- Schedule E—salaries and stock ownership of corporate officers.
- Schedule K—income that would be taxable to the corporation if it were a C corporation; distributions to stockholders; a Schedule K-1 for each stockholder.
- Schedule L—beginning and ending balance sheets.
- Schedule M—reconciliation of corporate books to tax return.

Two recent private Letter Rulings (8542034; 8544011) indicate that an S corporation shareholder must pick up his or her share of undistributed S corporation income on a current basis and include it in the computations of quarterly estimated tax. It is clear that a Sub S shareholder, like a partner, is not permitted to wait until the end of the year to take the undistributed income into account in determining estimated tax liability.

C corporations are required to make quarterly payments of estimated corporate taxes, on Form 1120W, for all quarters in which estimated corporate tax is $40 or over. That makes it fairly inevitable. The corporate quarterly filing dates are different from the individual quarterly filing dates: the 1120W's are due on or before the fifteenth day of the fourth, sixth, ninth, and twelfth months of the taxable year.

The C corporation annual return (the counterpart of the individual 1040) is the 1120, due on or before the fifteenth day of the third month after the end of the taxable year. The 1120 calls for gross income, deduction, and tax calculations, and it includes:

- Schedule A—cost of goods sold.
- Schedule C—dividends *received* by the corporation in its capacity as stockholder (dividends *paid* to the corporation's own stockholders are reported on Form 1096 no sooner than the last dividend payment of the year, no later than the last day of February of the year following the payment; each stockholder who receives over $10 in dividends gets a 1099-DIV, and copies of all the 1099-DIVs are attached to the 1096).
- Schedule E—salaries paid to officers.
- Schedule F—bad debts.
- Schedule J—computation of tax due.
- Schedule L—opening and closing balance sheets.
- Schedule M—reconciliation of tax and accounting treatment of items.

The form for a proprietor's, partner's, or S corporation stockholder's amended return in 1040X; the corporate amended return is the 1120X. Refunds can be expedited by attaching forms 1045 (for the 1040X) or 1139 (1120X). An automatic four-month extension for filing a 1040 or 1120S can be obtained by filing Form 4868 on or before the due date of the return; an automatic three-month extension for filing Form 1120 can be obtained on similar terms via Form 7004. *PRACTICE TIP: Part of the attorney's educational burden is the task of teaching the client the difference between an extension of time to file and additional time to pay. The latter is discretionary with the IRS, and much more difficult to obtain.*

State and Local Taxes: Most states impose a franchise tax on the privilege of doing business within the state, a corporate income tax, or both. It is more than likely that quarterly estimated payments will be required.

There may also be occupation taxes, unincorporated business taxes, chain store taxes, permit fees, and other taxes imposed at the state and/or local levels. The CCH state tax service is a very useful resource for the practitioner. In the end, though, the attorney advising a start-up business will have to consult the state code (try under Business and Professions and Corporations as well as under Revenue), the state administrative code, and the ordinances of the city or county.

Retailers face the additional problem of sales tax compliance. It is simplicity itself to get a sales tax number. Just write to the taxing authority or appear at its offices and a certificate will be issued, and a set of returns will be mailed to the business monthly or annually until an officer indicates that the business has been terminated.

The sales tax number also permits the business to purchase goods for resale without paying sales tax to the supplier. This provision is frequently misunderstood and frequently deliberately abused; few retailers check whether goods have been purchased for resale, for use in business but not for resale (e.g., office supplies for a garment retailer), or for personal use.

Sales taxes must be collected on intrastate sales by retailers doing business within the state. Thus, sales taxes need not be collected by a Minnesota company on mail-order sales made to New York customers and shipped to Arkansas from the warehouse in Minnesota. (If the company had a warehouse in New York, it would come within the sales tax jurisdiction of New York State.) Nor must sales taxes be collected on orders placed in one state for delivery to another neighboring state.

Both these provisions cost states a great deal of revenue and have occasioned understandable resentment. Legislation is now pending before Congress to require collection of other states' sales taxes and remission of these taxes to the appropriate authority; the resentment of retailers at the prospect is also understandable. In theory, anyone who buys goods out of state is obliged to pay use tax to the home jurisdiction—but anyone who believes that that happens in the real world must also be a "Brooklyn Bridge Buyer" and "Easter Bunny believer."

Employment Taxes and Tax Withholding

If the business will have any common-law employees, provisions must be made for tax compliance. (It may be possible to avoid having common-law employees if the entrepreneurs and their families can do all the work themselves; if all the work they can't do is handled by independent contractors; or if all employees are leased or hired from a temporary agency, so that the leasing or temporary agency, rather than the start-up business, is the employer and assumes the employer's burdens—subject to the tighter rules of the Tax Code of 1986.)

The business will be responsible for paying Workers' Compensation insurance premiums, at a rate ranging from about half of one percent to 51 percent of an employee's salary, depending on the state and on the inherent risk of the employee's duties. Information on rates and procedures can be gotten from the state Workers' Comp authorities—usually called the State Accident Insurance Fund or something similar.

The employer makes all the payments of FUTA (federal unemployment tax) and state unemployment tax. The basic FUTA rate is 6.2% of the first $7,000 of employee compensation, but a credit for state unemployment taxes is available up to 5.4%. State rates are adjusted based on the employer's "experience" of unemployment—that is, on the number of employees discharged and the length of time they collect benefits before returning to work.

The employer must both pay and collect FICA (Social Security) taxes, and must withhold federal income tax. Most states and some cities also have income taxes requiring withholding, and the business may have to be advised about how to withhold taxes for workers who live in one jurisdiction and work in another. An EIN (Employer Identification Number) is required for FICA and tax withholding purposes. The number can be obtained by either an incorporated or unincorporated business by filing Form SS-4 with the nearest IRS district office.

Usually, the IRS will mail a supply of Form 501 for making required deposits of withheld and employer-paid taxes when the employer gets its EIN; if it doesn't, forms should be available at the district office. Although it is not a legal necessity that the business open separate accounts for tax money, it is a highly recommended practice. Many businesses have been shut down by the IRS and many employers have been subjected to the statutory 100% penalty because of honest (or dishonest) mistakes and innocent or disingenuous confusion between the business's own, spendable money and sums already belonging to the IRS and the Social Security system.

The problem of compliance with employment taxes has two aspects: notification to the employee, and collection and deposit of taxes due. When employees are hired, it is up to the employer to get a W-4 form identifying the number of withholding exemptions the employee claims. (Withholding is not required if the W-4 indicates no tax liability for the preceding year and no anticipated tax liability for the current year.) Based on this number of exemptions, the employer withholds federal tax. There are two basic methods for doing this: the wage bracket and percentage method of withholding. The employer can get withholding tables directly from the IRS or from stationery stores.

Every year, the employer must prepare a W-2 form for each employee, giving his or her name, address, Social Security number, total wages, and the amount withheld, plus the employer's name, address, and EIN. The employee is entitled to get two copies of the W-2 on or before January 31 of each year (because the employees are almost certain to be calendar-year taxpayers, the requirement is geared to their tax year, not the employer's). It is courteous to provide a third copy if the employee must pay city as well as state and federal tax. The employer must file a copy of each W-2 with the IRS and another with the Social Security Administration by February 28 of each year.

Each independent contractor who receives $600 or more in compensation must be given a 1099-NEC [non-employee compensation], and the IRS also gets a copy; all 1099-NECs, as well as all other 1099 information returns, must be submitted to the IRS with a covering Form 1096 [summary of information returns] on or before the due date for the business's tax return.

FUTA and employer-paid FICA must be paid at least once a year on or before February 10. The form for FUTA is the 940; if FICA amounts are owed, the Form is 941, or 941E if nothing is owed over and above the amounts already deposited.

Deposits of employer-paid taxes and taxes withheld from employee compensation can be made to any bank, savings and loan, or credit union approved by the IRS. (The institution should be able to provide this information.) Depending on the total of FICA, FUTA, and withheld taxes, deposits may be required anywhere from quarterly to eight times a month.

Family Hiring Advantages: In addition to the joys of working with one's family and providing early business training for the next generation who may inherit the business, putting family members on the payroll has undeniable tax advantages.

As long as the compensation paid is paid in return for services actually rendered and the rate of compensation is reasonable (for example, naming a two-year-old son as the firm's comptroller is overreaching), a corporation is entitled to a deduction for compensation paid to family members. Young family members may not be subject to income tax at all; their bracket is likely to be lower than the corporation's bracket.

Putting one's spouse on the payroll does not provide any advantages of income-splitting as long as a joint return is filed. However, the entrepreneur and now-working spouse will be able to take an IRA deduction of $4,000 (as long as each earns at least $2,000, and as long as they are not participants in a qualified plan). Furthermore, a business owner's spouse and children under 21 are not treated as "employees" for FICA or FUTA purposes—another saving to the business (though the family members must pay Social Security taxes at the higher, self-employed rate).

Tax Accounting Considerations in Start-Ups

In some contexts, not to decide is to decide. A business that fails to adopt a fiscal year generally is obliged to use a calendar year unless it gets IRS approval for a change (and, as we've seen, partnerships and S corporations need IRS approval to adopt a fiscal year at all). Once a corporation adopts an accounting method (e.g., cash, accrual) and an inventory valuation method (e.g., LIFO), IRS permission will be required for a change. So the business must adopt tax accounting conventions suitable for the immediate needs of the start-up and that can be anticipated to fit the business's later needs.

Reg. §1.446-1(a)(4) requires all taxpayers to maintain accounting records enabling them to file a correct return each year; Reg. §1.6000-1(a) obligates taxpayers to keep permanent books of account or records, including inventories, sufficient to establish the amount of gross income, deductions, credits, and other items shown on the return. The standards for computerized accounting systems are found in Rev. Proc. 64-12, 1964-1 CB 672 and Rev. Rul. 71-20, 1971-1 CB 392. The age of these rules shows that the IRS hasn't really caught up with the computer revolution when it comes to taxpayers' accounting systems.

The Tax Year: The basic rule is that the taxpayer's taxable year must conform to the accounting year on which the business books are regularly kept [Code §441(c)]. If there aren't any books or if the books do not reflect an acceptable fiscal year, the taxpayer must pay taxes on a calendar-year basis [§441(g); *MacLean*, 73 TC 1045 (1980)].

Unless the taxpayer uses a 52-53 week year, any fiscal year adopted must end on the last day of the last month of the fiscal year. A taxpayer who adopts any other day as the end of the fiscal year must be a calendar-year taxpayer. The IRS is quite serious about this: Rev.Rul. 85-22, 1985-10 IRB 5, for instance, deals with the case of the taxpayer who starts up on a date other than the first of the month, then adopts a fiscal year ending exactly twelve months later.

This eminently sensible procedure is condemned by the IRS. The taxpayer's year is not a fiscal year, because it doesn't end on the last day of a month. Therefore, the taxpayer must either file an amended calendar year return or get IRS approval to switch to a conventional fiscal year. *PRACTICE TIP: Many state corporation statutes include a provision for delaying official incorporation until a date selected by the incorporators. It may be worthwhile to do this in order to have the official start-up date on the first of a month if fiscal-year operation is desired.*

IRS approval is not required for a C corporation to adopt a conventional fiscal year [Reg. §1.441-1(b)(3)].

A 52-53 week year (frequently used by retailers) always ends on the same day of the *week*—either the last Wednesday (or other chosen day) in the month, or the chosen day nearest to the last day of the calendar month. Code §441(f) allows a taxpayer who keeps books by this method to compute taxable income on that basis. But once a 52-53 week year is chosen, it must be adhered to until the IRS gives permission for a change. Reg. §1.441-2(c)(1) and (2) instruct the taxpayer adopting a 52-53 week year to attach a statement to the first return, giving the calendar month in which the year ends; the day of the week on which it ends; and whether the last chosen day of the month, or the chosen day closest to the end of the month, that will close each fiscal month.

Accounting Methods: A taxpayer must pay taxes based on the accounting method used to keep the books, in a fashion consistent from year to year [Reg. §1.446-1(a)(2)]. The accounting method must also clearly reflect the taxpayer's income and outgo. If the taxpayer doesn't use any method consistently, or chooses a method that distorts income or misallocates deductions, the IRS has the right to recompute the taxpayer's taxable income according to its own standards of clear reflection of income [Code §446(a)].

Several methods of accounting are accepted by the IRS for use under proper circumstances:

- Cash (the Tax Code of 1986 limits the use of the Cash Method by C corporations)
- Accrual
- Installment
- Completed contract
- Any hybrid method that is consistent and clearly reflects income.

The IRS also has the right to allow other accounting methods.

The cash basis is the simplest accounting method. Cash and property received are included in income in the year they are actually or constructively received (that is, a cash-basis taxpayer cannot defer reporting income once the income is available and can be reached by the taxpayer's own actions). Deductions are taken in the year the expense was actually paid. These rules obtain no matter when the income or expense was earned or incurred.

Accrual-basis taxpayers report income in the year in which the right to it first becomes fixed and the amount of income can be determined with reasonable accuracy; expenses are reported in the year in which they are accrued. Businesses with inventory (e.g., manufacturers; retailers) *must* use the accrual method for their purchases and sales (though not necessarily for other accounting items such as employee salaries and pensions) unless the IRS authorizes the use of another method [Reg. §1.446-1(c)(2)(i)]. Furthermore, if the production, purchase, and/or sale of merchandise are income-producing factors for the business, the business's beginning and ending inventory on hand (including finished goods, work in process, raw materials, and supplies) must be taken into account in computing the business's taxable income [Reg. §1.446-10(a)(4)(i)].

Except for certain small construction contracts, all long-term contracts (i.e., those requiring over two years to complete) entered into after 2/18/86 must follow one of the two methods prescribed by the Tax Code of 1986. Either the taxpayer must include revenues from the contract each year, based on the percentage of total contract costs incurred during that year (while deducting costs as they are actually encountered); or the taxpayer must take into account 40% of items as described above, and must apply its usual accounting method for the remaining 60%.

Reserves: Good accounting practice requires businesses to maintain reserves for certain disagreeable events that may occur (e.g., losing or settling suits, replacement of damaged equipment, returns of goods that have been sold). These reserves can be either funded (a separate account, containing actual money, has been established) or unfunded (the reserve is a pure book entry). However, in a departure from the usual rule that tax accounting must mirror the business's other accounting treatment, the IRS will permit deduction of reserves only if a specific deduction is authorized by the Code (e.g., bad debts, depreciation, amortization).

PRACTICE TIP: Consult the 1986 Code for changes in the way bad debts may be charged off.

Inventory Valuation: A business's taxable income not only depends in large part on its gross income, but also on the cost of goods sold. Therefore, the question of how inventory will be valued is one of the most important questions in business tax law.

Inventory can be valued at its cost, or at the lower of its cost or the market price. Whichever of these is elected, it should be applied consistently from year to year [Reg. §1.471-2(b)].

But which items have been sold out of a constantly fluctuating inventory? Assuming for the moment that items are valued at cost, what happens if some of the inventory items were purchased for $1 apiece, the rest at $1.25? The normal convention, which is used unless the business elects to reverse it [Reg. §1.471-2(d)], is FIFO—First in, First out. That is, it is assumed that the oldest items in inventory (which, in the real world, are apt to be the least expensive) are sold first.

Any taxpayer with inventory may elect LIFO (Last In, First Out) treatment [Reg. §1.471-1(a)]. Small businesses (average gross receipts under $5 million) can also use a simplified dollar-value LIFO method added by the Tax Code of 1986. Under LIFO, which mandates valuation at cost (not at the lower of cost or market), the last items purchased are deemed to be the first sold. The result is that the value of the inventory tends to remain fixed (reflecting earlier price levels) because the later-purchased goods, with fluctuating prices, are deemed sold.

LIFO usually has a good effect on the business's tax return (because it increases the cost of goods sold and therefore lowers taxable income) but a bad effect on its financial statements (because income, earnings and profits, and return on investment and equity are depressed). So the choice to elect or forgo LIFO depends on whether the business needs tax deductions more than it needs a set of financial statements that will cheer up present stockholders and attract future stockholders.

If the business does decide to make the LIFO election, it is done by filing Form 970, Application to Use Lifo Inventory Method, with the return for the first year in which LIFO is used. The election, once made, is irrevocable unless the IRS approves the change back. (Form 3115 is used to request changes in accounting method, including inventory valuation method.) The LIFO election must include an analysis of all the taxpayer's inventories for the beginning and end of the tax year and the beginning of the preceding tax year (if there was a preceding tax year), and a statement of how costs were computed for raw materials, goods in process, and finished goods.

Under certain circumstances, a business can overcome the FIFO presumption without electing LIFO, and can use a valuation method based on the average cost of goods sold. However, this method must be used consistently. Retailers can use the "retail inventory method" described in Reg. §1.471-8; to use this method, closing inventory is adjusted to find an approximate cost figure by factoring out the average markup on the goods involved.

The attorney and/or accountant for the start-up business must counsel the business founders about their accounting options and their tax consequences. They must make sure that the business has an easy-to-use accounting system that provides the information needed for tax compliance and that can be accessed easily when returns must be prepared.

The Home-Office Deduction

For start-ups of modest dimensions, the home of one of the business's founders may be the only business premises; a business founder who is an employee of a business organized in corporate form may take the position that, although the business furnishes him or her with an office outside the home, a home office is also a necessity.

The home-office deduction is one of the most amended sections of the Code, and has given rise to a high volume of litigation. The Tax Code of 1986's version of Code Section 280A, permits a deduction for home offices falling into one of these five categories:

1. the business's principal place of business
2. a place of business used to meet clients or customers in the ordinary course of business
3. a separate structure used in connection with a trade or business—for example, a garage used to invent computers
4. space used for inventory storage
5. day care facilities

If your client has several businesses, he or she is entitled to a deduction for a separate place of business for each (provided that the different places of business really exist).

The home-office deduction is available only for separate areas of the home. The clearest case is a separate structure or a room that is used only for business; part of a room or an alcove *may* qualify, though litigation may be required to establish this. It is clear that the deduction is not available if a taxpayer uses a multipurpose room for business, for instance, if she prepares corporate accounts in the family's living room. Furthermore, the claimed home office must be used on a regular basis.

The deduction is computed on the basis of floor space and number of days used. For example, if the business starts in July and uses 10% of the floor space of the taxpayer's home, the maximum deduction is 5% of the expenses of maintaining the house or apartment. There is an additional limitation on the deduction: it may not exceed the taxpayer's net income derived from the business: that is, gross income minus deductible business expenses that are *not* related to the use of the home office (e.g., a secretary's salary; postage and office supplies). However, this limitation does not apply to deductions that would be available with or without a home office (i.e., mortgage interest; real estate taxes). But your clients should not despair: the new Code allows excess home office expenses to be carried forward. Prior law did not permit this.

An employee (for example, a stockholder-employee of a corporation) is permitted a home-office deduction if the office is a necessity for the convenience of the employer (not merely if the employee finds it convenient to take work home and do it in a separate part of the home). TIP: To bolster the taxpayer's case, have the corporation give the employee a letter specifying that the home office is required by the corporation as a condition of employment, and that the corporation needs the employee to maintain the office for business reasons.

Thin Incorporation

Thinner is a very viable strategy for many start-up corporations. A "thin" incorporation is one in which the corporation sells very little stock or related equity instruments. Instead, the corporation gets most of its capital from loans—very likely from shareholders, officers, and directors rather than banks or outsiders.

This strategy has many advantages. For one, people who would be unwilling to buy stock in an untested corporation may be quite willing to become its creditors, because they know they can enforce the debt. For another, a corporate "insider" must pay tax at ordinary income rates on compensation, interest received, and dividends alike; it is a matter of indifference to the insider how the sums are characterized. And yet another advantage: a stockholder has to pay capital gains tax if he or she realizes part of his or her investment by selling stock at a profit; return of amounts loaned is tax free. But the corporation is entitled to deduct interest payments and compensation; however, it cannot deduct dividends. If the corporation faces a potential tax on excess retained earnings, it can point to the existence of a heavy debt load as a good reason for retaining earnings.

The IRS can re-characterize alleged debt as equity. If the anorexic corporation is also an S corporation, the so-called debt may really be a second class of stock, terminating the Subchapter S election. (See page 20 for a discussion of the "straight debt" safe harbor for S corporations.)

Here are some guidelines for distinguishing between real debt and disguised equity instruments:

- Real debt is evidenced by a properly drawn instrument
- the corporation treats it as debt for accounting purposes

- regular payments of principal and interest are made—it is suggestive of equity if the "creditors" make no attempt to collect if the corporation defaults on the "debt"
- subordination to the business's general creditors is suspicious
- if the corporation's assets and prospects make repayment according to the terms of the "note" unreasonable, the debt characterization is dubious
- if the so-called lending took place in proportion to the holdings of the various stockholders, the debt characterization is extremely doubtful
- contingent interest or provisions for deferral of payment in bad years are not necessarily proof of equity status, but it looks a lot better if the interest obligation is not contingent on the corporation's financial health.

As a very rough rule of thumb, a 3:1 debt equity ratio should be acceptable to the IRS; much higher ratios have been upheld, where the obligation was properly drafted and treated by all parties like an ordinary, arm's-length loan arrangement. IRS characterization of the debt: equity ratio also depends on the industry. A 5:1 ratio has been rejected in a lumber business [*Wood Preserving Corp. of Baltimore, Inc. v. Commissioner*, 347 F2d 117 (4th Cir. 1965)], and a 20,000:1 ratio has been accepted for an asphalt manufacturer [*Byerlite Corp. v. Williams*, 286 F2d 285 (6th Cir. 1960)]. A debt: equity ratio that would otherwise be unacceptably high may also be justified by a corporation's prospect of future earnings—high-risk, high-return businesses like oil drilling frequently carry a lot of debt without necessarily having the "debt" reclassified as equity because business realities dictate heavy debt.

Under Code §385, the IRS has the power to set debt-equity guidelines, and Proposed Regulations were issued; however, after several postponements of effective date, they were withdrawn in November of 1983. In the absence of Regulations, lawyers who counsel businesses must look to the case law. The IRS and the courts tend to consider the debt-equity problem from four perspectives: (1) assessing the parties' intentions [but a taxpayer's self-serving statements can't turn equity into debt: *In re James Lane*, 742 F2d 1311 (11th Cir. 1984), involving eleven unsecured demand notes issued by an S corporation to a major stockholder]: (2) the form and substance of the transaction ; (3) whether a business purpose was present for the choice of debt over equity capitalization; and (4) the economic realities of the transaction.

The case of *Bauer v. Commissioner*, 84-2 USTC ¶9996 (9th Cir. 1984) holds that the most meaningful ratio in this context is the ratio of total corporate liability to stockholders' equity (including both initial paid-in capital and retained earnings.) *Bauer* also lists factors to be considered in characterizing alleged debt as equity:

1. intent of the parties
2. the names given to the certificates—e.g., debentures vs. stock certificates
3. the absence or presence of a fixed maturity date
4. the source of payments

5. the "creditor's" right to enforce payments of interest and principal
6. whether the "creditor" is on terms of equality with, or subordinate to, unrelated creditors of the corporation
7. adequacy of the corporation's capitalization
8. identity of interest between creditor and stockholder
9. corporation's ability to get loans from non-stockholders
10. whether interest payments come from funds that would normally be used to pay dividends

For instance, when a corporation was in severe financial trouble and it would have taken a miracle for the "lender" (who owned 62% of the corporation's stock) to be repaid, the 42 advances of credit he made within a year were treated as contributions to the corporation's capital [*Roth Steel Tube Co.*, TC Memo 1985-58]. Similarly, so-called debt was characterized as equity by the 11th Circuit in *Stinnett's Pontiac Service Inc. v. Commissioner*, 730 F2d 634 (1984). There was no fixed maturity date; although the "notes" provided for 8% interest, only part of the alleged debt was evidenced by notes, and no interest payments were ever made. There was no reasonable expectation of payment, because repayment was at the discretion of the corporation and its brother corporation.

In short, the presence of one or more suspicious factors may result in the treatment of certain amounts intended as loans to a thin corporation as equity. This is especially likely if the so-called lender is an officer or major stockholder of the corporation (or if he or she is a spouse or relative of an officer or major stockholder).

One possibility would be for the thin corporation to look to loans from banks and other independent lenders. However, in practical terms, such loans nearly always require personal guarantees, because the banks don't want to rely on the credit of a start-up corporation. That leads us to the next problem: the tax effect of guarantees of corporate obligations made by corporate "insiders."

Loan Guarantees

The tax risk is that a loan made by an outsider (e.g., a bank) to the corporation, guaranteed by a shareholder (or a spouse or relative of a shareholder) will be treated as if the loan were really made to the shareholder, who then used the loan proceeds as a contribution to the corporation's capital. This is especially true if the corporation was thinly capitalized [*Smyers*, 57 TC 189 (1971)] and if the corporation couldn't have gotten the loan without the guarantee [*Datamation Services, Inc.*, TC Memo 1976-252]. The risk is less if the corporation was in stable financial condition when the loan was obtained, and only unforeseen financial conditions brought the guarantee into play [*Ripson*, TC Memo 1979-394].

The consequence of this treatment is that the shareholder who is called upon to pay up under the guarantee will be denied a bad-debt deduction: after all, one of the risks of stock ownership is the possibility of losing money. [See *In re James*

Lane, 742 F2d 1311 (11th Cir. 1984) (S corporation shareholder's amounts paid under loan guarantee treated as capital contributions).]

The case of *Donald Lee Atkinson,* TC Memo 1984-378 highlights the interaction between the thin incorporation and loan guarantee rules. The taxpayer and a business associate each contributed $250 to raise the statutory minimum capital required by the state; each received a 50% interest in the business. The rest of the capitalization for the business came from bank loans: an initial loan of $10,000, then a second loan of $65,000. That the taxpayer, rather than the corporation, was the real borrower was highlighted by the fact that the notes were rewritten with the taxpayer as the debtor of record.

The taxpayer was required to pay $23,000 pursuant to his guarantees; he claimed an ordinary loss of $75,000 as a business bad debt. The IRS denied the deduction. The Tax Court upheld the IRS. In the Tax Court's analysis, the taxpayer was the real borrower, and the alleged loan proceeds were contributions to capital; therefore, the payments under the guarantee were entitled to capital loss, but not ordinary loss, treatment.

Hobby Losses

The "hobby loss" problem raised by Code Section 183 is purely a problem of proprietorship, partnership, and S corporation businesses. C corporations are presumed to be in business for the purpose of making a profit (whether or not this presumption comes true in the real world).

Code Section 183 sets a limit on loss deductions available for "activities not engaged in for profit." Losses are deductible only up to the extent of gains. (Note that any profit produced accidentally in the course of an activity not engaged in for profit is fully taxable.) The deduction limit applies at the partnership level, so hobby losses can't be passed through to the partners: [Rev.Rul. 77-320, 1977-2 CB 78; *Brannen,* 78 TC #33 (1982)]. This is also true at the S corporation level [Reg. §1.183-1(f)].

As the term "hobby loss" suggests, the intent of Section 183 is to prevent taxpayers from deducting the costs of some enjoyable and expensive activity, claiming that it is a business that regrettably has yet to become profitable. However, there's a risk that a business (especially a part-time or sideline business) may be treated as a hobby if, despite the best efforts of its owners, profits are not forthcoming. An activity is presumed to be engaged in for profit if it shows a profit for any three or more of five consecutive years (two of seven consecutive years for horse breeding, showing, or training) [§183(d)].

PRACTICE TIP: *If you have a proprietorship, partnership, or S corporation as a client, you might advise the management about the effect of this provision, and the possible desirability of reversing the usual tax planning procedures.* That is, it may be worthwhile to accelerate income and defer deductions for three of the business's early years in order to safeguard the availability of loss deductions for the start-up years. Getting the business into the black quickly will also improve the availability of loans and equity investments.

Reg. §1.183-2 adopts an "objective" approach: what counts is the taxpayer's profit-making objective in entering or staying with the venture, whether or not he or she had a reasonable expectation of profit [*Fisher*, TC Memo 1980-183]. The Regulation lists the following nine factors for assessing the taxpayer's objective:

1. The manner in which the activity was conducted.
2. The taxpayer's expertise (or that of his or her advisors).
3. Time and effort spent on the activity.
4. Expectation that assets used in the activity would appreciate in value over time.
5. The taxpayer's record in similar activities—either a novice or a three-time loser is in a worse position than a person with a good track record.
6. The taxpayer's general financial picture. Does the activity seem intended as a major source of family income, or is entirely discretionary income being used?
7. The history of income or loss in the activity.
8. Amount of earnings—oil drilling quite reasonably absorbs more funds than printing programs for the church choir recital.
9. Pleasure or recreation element. It is very likely that a service rating yacht harbors has a hobby element; hardly anyone goes into the plumbing supplies business for glamor and excitement.

The possible application of the hobby loss provisions (like the possibility of piercing the corporate veil and the thin incorporation and loan guarantee rules) is a good reason for small businesses to be careful about observing the formalities of business organization; to maintain excellent contemporary records; and to get good professional advice about all technical areas in which the business owners are not expert.

5

PRACTICAL TASKS IN REPRESENTING THE START-UP BUSINESS

The lawyer for a start-up business frequently has more business experience and savvy than the would-be entrepreneurs. So he or she must provide advice and counsel on issues outside the strict bounds of incorporation. For instance, it is likely that the business will have some kind of rented business premises (if this is not the case, see pages 61–62 for the tax treatment of the home office), so the attorney's help will be needed in negotiating, or at least reviewing, the commercial lease. Furthermore, unless the initial owners of the business are prepared to furnish all the start-up capital themselves, money must be raised: in the form of loans and/or stock sales. Loans must be negotiated and the agreements reviewed; stock sales are subject to intensive state and federal regulation. If a venture capitalist is involved, the terms on which capital will be made available must be considered. The corporation—with help from the lawyer—must decide on the appropriate balance between debt and equity financing, and must conform with the tax rules on thin incorporation.

Commercial Leases

Clients who want to start businesses sometimes think that they're familiar with commercial leases just because they've served time as apartment tenants. But the residential lease (though not without its own problems of interpretation) is simplicity itself compared with the commercial lease. Furthermore, many localities provide at least some protection for the residential tenant against eviction and rent increases; residential leases are usually written for a flat rate during the term; and it is unusual indeed for a residential tenant to have to contribute a portion of his or her income, in addition to the stated rent, to the landlord. Commercial tenants have little or no protection against escalator clauses, announcements that the rent will triple when the lease expires, and other landlordly pleasantries. So the sensible entrepreneur will involve his or her attorney in the process of negotiating for commercial space.

If the particular area in which the business will be started has an oversupply of rental space, the business owners may be able to obtain substantial concessions in terms. But in the more usual situation where space is scant (especially space in areas with heavy foot and walk-in traffic, close to public transportation and/or parking, and accessible to deliveries), the tenant will not be able to make many changes in the lease terms, but at least can understand them and face rent escalation philosophically and without surprise.

Residential tenants can usually distinguish between a two-room and a three-room apartment but first-time commercial tenants are unlikely to be familiar with "loss factors," the difference between the amount of space advertised (e.g., 1,500 square feet) and the amount that can actually be used by the tenant. *PRACTICE TIP: The conventional definition of rentable space is the entire amount contained within the building's interior walls, with the exception of the core space containing the elevators and related services. But the space for rent may not be rectangular—there may be bays reducing the usable space; there may also be pillars, electrical installations, and other items limiting use of the space.*

If your client is seriously interested in a particular space, it probably pays to have an architect or engineer inspect and measure the space, and explain any constraints on use (e.g., all the electric outlets are along one wall; there's only one telephone jack, you can't get to the men's room without walking through what's supposed to be the president's office).

From the tenant's point of view, the best lease is long term and has liberal sublet clauses. From the landlord's point of view, the best lease is either very long (if tenants are scarce on the ground) or very short (if "gentrification" is underway and an ice-cream store can be persuaded to pay three times the rent for the same space). As a balance between these needs, the average commercial lease has escalator clauses permitting the landlord to raise the rent on the occurrence of a number of quite common conditions. There may be some negotiating room here, or the lease may be on a take-it-or-leave-it basis. But at least the tenant can make meaningful comparisons among several potential business spaces: the one with the highest initial stated rate may offer the largest amount of usable space (because the landlord's calculation is closest to reality) and the lowest actual rate in practice (because it has the smallest potential for rent escalation).

The typical escalator clauses (which may occur in combination) include:

- "Porter's wage adjustment." *PRACTICE TIP: check the definition carefully; it may include all operating expenses of the building.*
- Operating expense escalation payments.
- Tax escalation payments—a particular favorite among landlords who can charge each of, say, ten tenants 15% of the tax increase.
- Parking area contributions.
- Increases based on increased utility rates—again, the landlord may make a few dollars on this one. Commercial buildings usually have a single meter, and the tenant's rent includes an allowance for electricity (though the lease may also include a provision for a surcharge for excessive use—though seldom a rebate for sedulous energy conservation). Sometimes each unit has a separate meter or the arrangement *may* be what is called "submetering," under which the landlord bills the tenant for usage—generally with a service charge.

Escalator clauses must also be examined to determine what the triggering event is. One provision sometimes encountered depends on the Consumer Price Index. But since the CPI includes an allowance for tax increases, the tenant gets hit twice if the lease also includes a tax increase clause; it may be possible to negotiate a reduction in the escalator clause to compensate for the duplication. It is also important to check the base year against which comparisons are made—it is not unheard of for the landlord to choose a remote past year of low costs, so that the escalation is correspondingly dramatic. It is understandable that tenants may wish a rent de-escalator clause if the landlord succeeds in getting a real estate tax rebate. Whether this can be achieved is a matter of negotiating power.

Leases in malls and shopping centers commonly include a provision that the tenant must pay a certain percentage of monthly income in addition to the stated rent. There may also be a requirement that the tenant join a tenant's association or pay assessments, to be used for general promotion and maintenance of the mall or shopping center.

Piercing the Corporate Veil

A lawyer, like any craftsman, likes to see a job well done. If the job of incorporating a start-up business is not done well, the corporation and its stockholders face the threat of "piercing the corporate veil": that is, the existence of the corporation may be disregarded and the stockholders will lose their limitation of liability, and will be fully liable for corporate debts as though they were partners rather than stockholders.

New York drafters should also be aware of BCL Section 630 which holds that, even in a properly formed corporation, the ten largest shareholders of a nonlisted company whose shares are not regularly traded over the counter are personally, jointly, and severally liable for the corporation's debts and the wages and salaries of employees. This gives them an incentive to see that the corporation is well-managed! It has been held that this statute, as it applies to unpaid contributions to the employees' pension and welfare funds, is not preempted by ERISA [*Sasso v. Vachris,* 54 LW 2250 (NY App. 1985)].

Outside of New York, states have varying standards for piercing the veil. A corporation should be immune if the appropriate formalities have been gone through (e.g., if the Articles of Incorporation were properly filed; a Certificate of Incorporation obtained from the Secretary of State or other appropriate authority; if an organization meeting was held, and directors elected unless the corporation elects to do without a Board of Directors; if annual meetings are held as provided by the Articles of Incorporation and/or bylaws; etc.) and if the corporation has an independent existence—it is not merely an alter ego of a single dominating individual or group.

Bucyrus-Erie Co. v. General Products Corp., 643 F2d 413 (6th Cir. 1981) gives a useful summary of the reasons for piercing the corporate veil, as follows:

- the corporation is so dominated by one or more stockholders as to have "no will of its own"
- this domination is used to commit dishonest or injust acts—for example, to obtain property for the stockholders' personal use, without paying for it
- the injury that is the occasion for piercing the corporate veil is a product both of the domination and of the wrongdoing.

One-person corporations and corporations that are successors of proprietorships or partnerships are particularly likely to encounter claims that the veil should be pierced—and thus, the lawyer counseling the business should be especially careful to handle the incorporation process properly and to instruct the client(s) as to the differences in the way they must do business in the future.

In particular, the stockholder(s) of the new corporation must beware of commingling personal and business funds [see *Honeywell, Inc. v. Arnold Construction Co. Inc.,* 134 Ariz. 153, 654 P2d 301 (1982); *U.S. v. Healthwin-Midtown Convalescent Hosp.,* 511 F.Supp. 416 (D.Cal. 1981)] and must be sure to maintain books and records in proper corporate form. *Rhode Island Hosp. Trust Nat'l Bank v. Almonte,* CCH Corp. Law. Guide ¶11,903 allows piercing of the corporate veil of a bankrupt corporation where a check-kiting operation was instituted by a corporate officer for his personal benefit. The owner of an incorporated art gallery was held personally liable for breaches of warranty as to the age and provenance of art objects in *Dawson v. G. Malina, Inc.,* 463 F.Supp. 461 (SDNY 1978). The corporate name was "merely the name used for the seller's art gallery"; no Board of Directors meetings had been held since the organization meetings; no minutes were kept; and only one corporate franchise tax report had been filed in several years of nominally corporate existence.

But if the corporation's existence is legitimate, the corporation's status will not be invalidated by continued use of the predecessor sole proprietorship's trade name; by continued use of materials printed before incorporation; or by a loan from the sole shareholder to the corporation [*Southwest Bank of Omaha v. Moritz,* 203 Neb. 45, 277 NW2d 430 (1979)].

Similarly, the partners-turned-stockholders in *Seymour v. Hull & Moreland Engineering,* 605 F2d 1105 (9th Cir. 1979) were not personally liable for alleged shortfalls in contributions to an employee trust created under a union contract with the partnership and continued after incorporation. The union trustee knew that the corporation was the partnership's successor and had accepted the corporation's checks. The *Hull* court refused to pierce the corporate veil because there was no commingling of personal and business funds, nor was the intent in incorporating fraudulent.

In some states, the major test is whether the stockholders themselves are guilty of fraud or illegal acts [see *United States National Bank of Omaha v. Rupe,* 207 Neb. 131, 296 NW2d 474 (1980); *Slusarski v. American Confinement Systems, Inc.,* CCH Corp. Law Guide ¶11,903 (Neb. Sup. Ct. 1984)]. However, fraud and wrongdoing were not required for piercing of the corporate veil in *Cunningham v. Rendez-Vous Inc.,* 51 LW 2542 (4th Cir. 1983) [a Death on the High Seas Act case]. In *Cunningham,* the tests were undercapitalization or disregard of corporate formalities, combined with an element of injustice or fundamental unfairness if the stockholders were not held individually liable.

Undercapitalization and commingling were important factors in the decision to pierce the veil in *Byrd v. Brand,* 140 Ga. App. 135, 230 SE2d 113 (1976) and *U.S. v. Healthwin-Midtown Convalescent Hospital, supra.* In *Byrd,* form letters on corporate stationery to all suppliers (including the plaintiff) were admitted to show that the plaintiff had notice of the corporation's existence. The standards for piercing the veil were given as fraud by the corporation's owner(s) and credit obtained on personal assumption of responsibility. The amount of corporate borrowing without personal responsibility was held inadmissable if the defendant's dealings with other creditors were not relevant to the instant case.

The individual defendant in *Healthwin-Midtown* was a nursing home's former president who owned 50% of its stock. The corporate veil was pierced because there was a unity of interest and ownership between the corporation and the individual; the corporation did not have a separate "personality"; and it would be inequitable to treat the corporation as a separate entity (actual fraud was not required). Corporate formalities were disregarded; the corporation was under-capitalized; and the individual defendant's personal finances were inextricably intertwined with the nursing home's finances and those of his other business interests.

The question of when a corporation is adequately capitalized is a difficult one (see a discussion of the tax implications of thin incorporation on pages 62–65). From the point of view of piercing the corporate veil, insolvency shortly after incorporation is at least a fair indication that the capitalization was inadequate [*Norris Chemical Co. v. Ingram,* 139 Ariz. 544, 679 P2d 567 (1984)].

In short, to avoid piercing of the corporate veil and individual liability of stockholders, the client must be aware of the need to incorporate in proper form; to hold meetings as required, and to maintain minutes of the meeting; and to inform creditors who dealt with the corporation before incorporation that its status has changed. The corporation must pay all necessary fees and taxes, and maintain appropriate books and records. The corporation must begin with and maintain adequate capitalization, and the stockholders must neither commit fraud or unfair transactions, nor commingle their personal finances with those of the corporation.

Licenses

This subject is so idiosyncratic that all I can do is give you a few words of general guidance. There are two major kinds of licenses required of businesses: police power licenses, imposed to protect the public (e.g., licensure of plumbers to avert the potential dangers caused by unskilled experimentation with pipes) and revenue licenses, imposed to raise some extra funds.

Licenses can be required at the state level (check the state's Business and Professions or Business and Occupations volume) or the county or city level (check the ordinances). New York City, for instance, requires retailers to register with the City's Department of Consumer Protection.

Other possible sources of information about licensing: the most current edition of Juvenal L. Angel's *Directory of Professional and Occupational Licensing in the United States* (Simon and Schuster); your state or city's office set up to provide assistance to small business; or the nearest SCORE (Service Corps of Retired Executives) office.

Annual Reports

All the states, except Pennsylvania, require regular reports to be filed by domestic corporations and by foreign corporations qualified to do business in the state. Usually, these reports are due annually, sometimes in conjunction with the franchise tax payment; however, some states (e.g., Alaska, Colorado, Connecticut) require only a biennial report.

An annual (or biennial) report generally calls for information such as in the following list that comes from §16.22 of the revised Model Business Corporation Act:

- the corporation's name
- the corporation's jurisdiction of incorporation
- the address of the corporation's registered office within the state, and the name of its registered agent
- the address of the corporation's principal office (if other than its registered office)

- names and business addresses of the corporation's directors and principal officers
- the nature of the corporation's business
- the authorized capitalization, analyzed by class and series
- the issued stock, analyzed by class and series

Some states also require an annual report to disclose the corporation's total assets, assets in state, gross sales, sales in state, or similar tax-related information.

Although filling out an annual (or biennial) report is not likely to be much of a burden, it is a small task that the corporation must never neglect: the various state statutes prescribe penalties ranging from fines to revocation of a foreign corporation's certificate of authority to involuntary dissolution of a domestic corporation if the report is not filed as required. Therefore, another task for the attorney is to inform the clients of this responsibility and how to carry it out.

Privacy, Attorney-Client Privilege, and the Fifth Amendment

It is necessary to be very tactful about this, because it is both a source of ethical problems and most inexpedient for an attorney to be aware of criminal activity or activity likely to result in litigation, which is contemplated by a client. However, it is reasonably clear that the Fifth Amendment protection against self-incrimination is purely a personal privilege, and cannot be claimed by a partnership or a corporation [*Bellis v. U.S.*, 417 US 85 (1974); *SEC v. Kingsley*, 510 F.Supp. 561 (D.D.C. 1981); *In re Grand Jury Proceedings (Morganstern)*, 54 LW 2133 (6th Cir. 1985)], although it may be claimed by a sole proprietorship, because the proprietorship is not an entity separate from its owner.

Therefore, the Fifth Amendment privilege against self-incrimination may be used in opposition to a *subpoena duces tecum* demanding production of a sole proprietorship's records [*U.S. v. Doe*, 52 LW 4296 (Sup.Ct. 1984)]. (However, a corporation *is* protected by the double jeopardy provisions of the Fifth Amendment: *U.S. v. Security National Bank*, 546 F2d 492 (2d Cir. 1976), *cert.den.* 430 US 950.) This may make a difference to the client in choosing a form of organization.

Corporations, however, are entitled to the attorney-client privilege, just as any other client is. The problem comes in determining the scope of the privilege. As a general rule, the privilege covers information imparted to an attorney so that he or she can render *legal* rather than *investigative* services [see *Osternick v. E.T. Barwick Industries*, 82 FRD 81 (ND Ga. 1979); *Diversified Industries Inc. v. Meredith*, 572 F2d 596 (8th Cir. 1978); *SEC v. Gulf & Western*, 518 F.Supp. 675 (D.D.C. 1981)]. There is a split in authority as to whether preparing tax returns constitutes legal work within the ambit of the attorney-client privilege. The Second Circuit says yes [*Colton v. U.S.*, 306 F2d 633 (1962), *cert.den.* 371 US 951]; the Fifth and Eighth Circuits say no [*U.S. v. Davis*, 636 F2d 1028 (5th Cir.1981); *Canady v. U.S.*, 354 F2d 849 (8th Cir. 1966)].

The work-product rule exempts from discovery materials prepared by an attorney for a trial or in anticipation of litigation—not merely because litigation is a remote possibility. But Federal Rules of Civil Procedure 26(b)(3) permits discovery of an attorney's work product where there is substantial need for the material, and the substantial equivalent information cannot be obtained without undue hardship—[see *U.S. v. Amerada Hess Corp.*, 619 F2d 980 (3d Cir. 1980)].

For examples of these rules in action, see *Alpha Beta Co. v. Sundy*, 157 Cal. App.3d 818 (1984) [corporate general counsel, who was also a Vice President of the corporation, was not required to give a deposition in a libel action, because the answers would disclose privileged communications]; *In re Dayco Corp.*, CCH Corp. Law Guide ¶11,964 (SD Ohio 1984) [report prepared by an attorney for a corporation charged with RICO and securities law violations was not discoverable in a derivative suit against the corporation even though a press release summarizing its contents had been published. The press release did not waive the attorney-client privilege because only the findings, not the evidence behind them, had been disclosed. However, a report prepared by an *accountant* was not privileged, and thus was discoverable]; *Pritchard-Keang Nam Corp. v. Jaworski*, CCH Federal Securities Law Reporter ¶91,930 (8th Cir. 1984) [investigative report prepared by an independent law firm dealing with allegedly questionable foreign payments was covered by the attorney-client privilege].

Depending on the activities the client intends to engage in, it may be sound planning to organize the business as a sole proprietorship rather than a partnership or corporation (if the attorney can't talk the client out of the questionable activities); and it may be more prudent to have tax returns and reports prepared by an attorney rather than an accountant, because the attorney-client relationship, unlike the accountant-client relationship, creates the possibility of work-product protection.

Franchises

The franchise form of operation gives a person with a profitable business (or at least a potentially profitable business idea) a chance to make commercial use of the idea by permitting others to take advantage of the business identity by using the same name and offering similar merchandise or services in a similar format. The franchisor (offering the franchise) gets to derive many of the benefits of operating in many business locations, while passing along much of the risk to the franchisees.

The franchisee, in turn, gets the advantage of local or nationwide advertising; high buyer recognition of the franchise name and/or trademark; and gets some measure of training and assistance with the day-to-day business tasks. Thus, franchising is attractive to a number of business novices who want to go into business but are uncertain of being able to attract enough customers to a free-standing operation.

PRACTICE TIP: The lawyer for the potential franchisee has to do a lot of educating, and must examine the franchise documents carefully. Franchisees must be aware of two potential dangers. First, franchising has attracted a number of unscrupulous franchisors, and the client must be protected against their blandishments. Fortunately, federal and state laws call for a high degree of disclosure, and careful examination of the franchise documents can often separate the law-abiding franchisor from the fly-by-nights.

The second, and much greater, risk is that franchising—even if the franchisor is successful, well-established, and entirely honest—is by no means an automatic passport to fortune. Although franchising diminishes some of the risks of doing business (by providing guaranteed—and sometimes mandatory—sources of supply for ingredients or inventory; by allowing the franchisee to benefit from the establishment of a strong trademark or corporate identity), many of the risks of doing business continue. The would-be franchisee will face competition from other franchises and from free-standing businesses. In fact, the franchisor may sell another franchise a few blocks away, so the franchisee finds himself competing against another "Good Ol'Granma's Oatmeal Cookie" outlet (or whatever). Due to excessive competition, decline in demand, increase in operating costs, or the franchisee's own inexperience or incompetence, the franchise may lose money.

Well-established franchises (e.g., McDonald's, Burger King) are very expensive, which can create substantial funding problems for the would-be franchisee. Furthermore, national franchises often require that much of the initial franchise fee be paid from the applicant's own resources, not financed.

Federally Mandated Disclosures: The Federal Trade Commission has promulgated a rule (16 CFR Part 436) mandating very extensive disclosure. (You can find the text in the CCH Trade Regulation Reporter at ¶38,029.) The FTC rule supersedes state laws that are less protective of potential franchisees, but not those that provide more protection or require further disclosure.

The FTC rule makes it an unfair or deceptive trade practice as defined by Section 5 of the FTC Act for the franchisor (or a franchise broker) to fail or refuse to provide potential franchisees with a prospectus and other disclosure documents. The franchisor must disclose information under 20 headings, including the following:

1. The name, address, principal place of business, trademarks, and names under which business is done, for the franchisor itself and any parent firm or holding company.

2. The business experience of the franchisor, its parent or holding company, and its directors and officers in the past five years.

3. Whether the franchisor, parent, officer, director, etc., has been found guilty or plead *nolo* to any charge of fraud, securities offenses, or the like, within the past seven years; whether they are the subject of any restrictive order issued by a federal agency (e.g., a cease and desist order); whether any of them has undergone bankruptcy or insolvency within the past seven years.

4. A factual description of the franchise offered.

5. Initial funds the franchisee must provide, for example,
   A. deposits
   B. initial fee
   C. down payments
   D. prepaid rent
   E. equipment and inventory

   The franchisor must also disclose if, and under what circumstances, such sums can be returned to the franchisee.

6. Recurring payments the franchisee must make, for example,
   A. training
   B. royalties and leases
   C. advertising
   D. sign rental

7. Whether the franchisee is required to do business with any affiliates of the franchisor, and whether the franchisee is required to buy, rent, or lease anything, and from whom. These two innocuous-sounding requirements generate endless friction between franchisors and franchisees, because franchisees are frequently required to buy food items, utensils, etc., from specified vendors who, in turn, are frequently affiliated with the franchisor. The franchisor maintains that the specifications are necessary to maintain a standard of quality throughout the franchise operation; the franchisees claim that they are forced to buy standard or inferior merchandise at inflated prices.

8. If the franchisor offers any financing, the material terms and conditions of the financing.

9. Extent of personal participation required of the franchisee. Are franchisees expected to devote full time to the franchise, or are they permitted to be passive investors or to use the franchise as a sideline business?

10. If a public figure's name is used in connection with the franchise, the extent of his or her participation.

11. If training will be offered, what it will consist of, and its cost to the franchisee.

12. The number of franchises in operation at the end of the preceding fiscal year (and how many of them were company-owned; the names and addresses of the ten nearest franchisees, and all of them in the franchisee's state; the number repurchased or terminated in the preceding fiscal year).

13. The length of the franchise agreement, conditions under which it can be renewed and conditions under which either party can terminate it.

14. The franchisor's balance sheet for the most recent fiscal year, and income statements for the current year and the two preceding years.

It is also a violation of Section 5 of the FTC Act for a franchisor to promise a particular level of sales, income, or profits, unless the statements are disclosed as estimates and unless they are reasonable and supported by evidence.

Other potential sources of franchisor-franchisee conflict arise when the franchisee is required to accept all new franchisor products (e.g., the Hulaburger, a one-time McDonald's specialty lamented by no one but Ray Kroc); when the franchisee is forbidden to adopt new, nonfranchise products; geographical restrictions on the territory in which the franchisee may do business; unavailability of additional franchise units if the franchisee wants to buy them; difficulty of terminating the franchise agreement on terms acceptable to the franchisee; franchisor's willingness to sell franchises close enough to compete with the franchisee; franchisee's obligation to pay heavy fees or high percentages of income to the franchisor; obligation to pay high advertising fees; obligation to use advertising and display materials or decorative schemes that the franchisee dislikes or feels are bad for business; obligation to maintain hours that the franchisee feels are too long or are poorly chosen; and insufficient training.

If the potential franchisee thoroughly understands the franchise agreement, the prospectus, and financial statements; if he or she has enough business experience and/or acumen to make a go of the business; if the franchise location is suitable for the type of business to be conducted; and if financing is available on terms that will not preclude profit, then franchising can be an excellent way for a person (particularly a business novice) to start a prospering business. The attorney can provide much of the information required for a successful franchise start-up.

Legal Problems of Particular Businesses

Some things are constant no matter what kind of business is being started up: there must be capital, a form of organization must be chosen, and records must be kept. But beyond that level of generality, each kind of business generates its own legal problems.

The following pages provide checklists of some of the issues that may arise in the creation of various kinds of businesses:

Problems of Manufacturers

- The business location must be zoned for manufacturing
- The location must be accessible to trucks making deliveries
- Shipping must be available
- Legal and inexpensive disposition of waste products must be available
- If work force is large, there is a strong possibility of an attempt at union organization
- The business's accounting system must be able to provide accurate inventory at least twice a year, and it must be able to account for raw materials, work in process, and completed manufactured goods
- Occupational safety and health laws must be complied with

- Liability insurance or self-insurance must be available in case toxic substances are accidentally discharged
- Liability insurance or self-insurance must be available against the possibility of claims made by end users of the products or others injured by the product
- Manufacturer should be aware of factoring and other forms of commercial financing
- Manufacturer should be aware of UCC remedies for merchant buyers and sellers (e.g., late delivery, noncomplying delivery, late payment)

Problems of Retailers

- An adequate network of suppliers must be created, preferably without creating exclusive relationships that limit the availability of merchandise or price negotiating flexibility
- Extensive (and expensive) security arrangements may have to be made before a carrier will provide burglary and other theft insurance
- A policy for dealing with suspected shoplifters must be set and reviewed by counsel to prevent unlawful detention, slander/libel, and abuse of polygraphs
- Liability insurance or self-insurance is needed—for slip-and-fall situations, etc.
- There may be restrictions on store decoration and displays imposed by developer (especially in a shopping mall)
- A mall tenant may have to join a tenants' association, pay advertising fees, percentage of profit to mall, etc.
- A retailer must collect state sales tax (if any) on sales of goods carried by customer, or for delivery to points within states, and must make required deposits and payments of sales tax (usually monthly, or quarterly if volume is small)
- A retail business may have to be registered with local consumer protection authorities
- If a retailer regularly permits payment in four or more installments of consumer purchases, the retailer must comply with Truth in Lending laws (e.g., must provide disclosure of amount financed, finance charge, and Annual Percentage Rate)
- If a retailer takes security interest in consumers' other property, Article 9 formalities regarding filing and perfection of security interest must be observed
- A retailer should be familiar with factoring and other forms of commercial finance
- A retailer should understand UCC provisions regarding merchant-to-merchant transactions

- A retailer must find out if local Blue Laws forbid or limit Sunday operations

Problems of Restaurants and Other Food Businesses

- Kitchens and kitchen equipment must conform to standards
- There is a need for frequent inspections
- There are packaging and labelling restrictions on packaged goods (e.g., it may be necessary to disclose ingredients, give sodium content, etc.)
- Restaurants with ten or more employees who regularly receive tips must comply with complex IRS procedures for withholding expected amounts of tip income
- The liquor license of the past restaurant owner may not be transferrable; a new liquor license may not be available because locality already has too many licensed premises, or because the restaurant location is too close to a church or school, or because parking is unavailable
- Heavy liability insurance may be required from possible claims of food poisoning; slip-and-fall; claims arising out of drunk driving by restaurant patrons if liquor is served

Problems of Service Businesses

- Depending on the state and service to be rendered, operation in PC form may be available
- Check state law for mutual responsibility of service providers for malpractice committed by fellow-providers
- There may be a need for malpractice insurance as well as premises liability, etc.
- Service providers, too, are subject to Truth in Lending if they regularly accept payment in four or more installments
- Depending on local law, a service business may be subject to unincorporated business tax (if not practiced in corporate form), and services may be subject to sales tax

EXAMPLES: To apply these principles to the examples discussed above, remember that Executive Perks and Hiroshi's enterprise (incorporated as Eastern Beautanicals Inc.—a cross between "beauty" and "botanicals") are both manufacturers. However, Eastern Beautanicals faces additional problems as a manufacturer of products used on the face and body. FDA approval may be required if the company offers "treatment" products, and liability exposure is much greater for a cosmetic company than for a manufacturer of coffee-makers. (However, the potential for liability if a coffee-maker explodes or if chemicals are leached into the coffee, is not inconsiderable.) Geneva Confections faces an even higher level of regulation because it sells food products. If it sells directly to the public, procedures must be developed for sales tax collection and remittance.

6

THE CORPORATE BALANCE OF POWER

The dynamics of the closely held corporation can have the inevitability—and the potential for all-around hassle—of a Greek tragedy. The typical corporation is started by a small group of people—often, an inventor; a sales-getter; and someone who takes care of the new company's books and records. Each of them invests something, and gets some stock in return for services. As the years go on, the business prospers, and it is necessary to add employees. Perhaps more stock will be issued, to raise additional capital.

The business then faces a number of potential obstacles. Once the business is off and running, it is common for the stockholders to be divided into two groups: those who are employed by the business and those who are not. The former group can benefit by dividends (and perhaps directors' fees, in the quite likely cases that they do serve on the Board, and that they are compensated for it) and the appreciation in value of their stock. But probably their main source of return on their investment in the corporation comes from their salaries, retirement plans, and other compensation.

The nonemployed group cannot realize any return on their investment in the corporation unless they receive dividends—and closely held businesses are notorious for failure to pay dividends (or, from management's point of view, for reinvesting profits for continued growth). Of course, they can sell their stock and get the benefit of its increased value, provided that they can find someone who wants to buy it; small-company stock is also notoriously illiquid.

At other times, the nonemployed shareholders (or minority shareholders who are employees) can threaten to upset the corporate apple cart: perhaps by destroying the Sub S election by selling their stock to a large number of buyers or to buyers who are ineligible to hold Sub S stock. (This tactic was especially effective when the S corporation was limited to 15 stockholders.) Or they can sell their 10% holding in Giuseppe's Pizza Parlors to arch-rival Giorgio's Pizza Parlors.

The voting patterns of small corporations are fascinating to aficionados of politics at its most brutal. Depending on the way the shares are held, a single shareholder may have an absolute majority at all times; or there may be a bloc of less-than-majority shareholders who together can always mobilize a majority; or there may be no single majority shareholder, but an ever-shifting series of alliances. Management and/or the majority stockholders (of course, the two groups are frequently identical in the small corporation) may continually be frustrated if blocs of minority stockholders continually veto their desired actions. Contrariwise, minority stockholders are subject to a variety of squeeze out devices denying them adequate return on their investment or adequate representation and profit if and when the corporation is merged or acquired.

The problems of the closely held corporation intensify in the second generation, and many such businesses flounder, not because the business lacks profit potential but because there is no method of passing the business on to a younger generation when the founder retires or dies. The second generation may have entirely different ideas about the conduct of the business, and may create vigorous conflict by pressing for diversification, vertical integration—or selling the business to a conglomerate because its internal rate of return, which is the pride and joy of the older generation, seems anemic to the "yuppie" stockholders. Or, the second generation may have no desire to be involved in the business at all, and may want to get rid of the illiquid stock in search of more conventional investments.

Corporation law has evolved a number of devices affecting the balance of power in the corporation. Your clients should be advised of all of them, and the desired devices should be adopted as part of the start-up process—either by including them in the Articles of Incorporation or bylaws, or through separate agreements. The devices include:

- the buy-sell agreement: a multi-purpose device that is very helpful in close corporations—and almost essential in partnerships, because there is almost no other way of liquidating a partnership interest on disability, retirement, or death

- transfer restrictions on close-corporation shares—so important that some state close-corporation statutes mandate transfer restrictions
- shareholder voting agreements
- shareholder voting trusts
- agreements among the shareholders, or between shareholders and corporations, about corporate governance
- preemptive rights
- cumulative voting

Buy-Sell Agreements

The buy-sell agreement can be drafted to serve a number of purposes: to provide liquidity to a shareholder's family or estate; to keep the stock within the original ownership group; to provide retirement funds for a shareholder; to create an estate at minimal cost by using insurance. Perhaps the most compelling reason: to set a value for closely held corporation stock that will be acceptable both to the stockholder and to the IRS; the valuation of close corporation stock is a perpetual trial. (Often literally—the issue has been litigated frequently.)

To sum up, the IRS is likely to accept a valuation set by a buy-sell agreement if the agreement also imposes transfer restrictions during life; if sale and purchase are mandatory at death; and if the price was fair when established, if the agreement was part of an arm's-length transaction, or both.

The essence of a buy-sell agreement is that each shareholder agrees that, on the selected triggering event(s)—retirement, disability, death—either the corporation or the other shareholders will buy his or her stock. If the corporation buys the stock, the agreement provides for an *entity purchase*; if the other stockholders do, it is a *cross-purchase* agreement. (Similar arrangements can be made for sale of partnership interests.)

Entity purchase agreements usually maintain the proportionate ownership of the survivors; cross-purchase can be set up that way, and can provide a different distribution.

The usual way of funding a buy-sell agreement is to use insurance. (Of course, this will work only for death and disability, not for retirement—retirement is not an insurable event.) Either the corporation or the fellow shareholders have an insurable interest in a shareholder's continued life and health, so there's no problem about securing the policies. In an entity purchase, the corporation (or partnership) buys a policy on the life of each of the participants, in an amount adequate to satisfy the buy-out obligation. In a cross-purchase, each participant maintains a policy on the life of each of the other participants—in a largish corporation or partnership, this can require a multiplicity of policies.

TIP: If some shareholders have much larger interests than the rest, they may resist an entity purchase. Why? Because a 60% shareholder will, in effect, be paying 60% of the premiums, but will wind up with far less than 60% of the stock when a fellow shareholder dies. On the other hand, if the buy-sell agreement takes the form of a cross-purchase, each stockholder will buy policies precisely large enough to cover his or her obligations to buy out other stockholders.

Transfer Restrictions

A corporation cannot out-and-out forbid *all* sales or transfers of its stock; that would be illegal as an unreasonable restraint on alienation. After all, one of the outstanding characteristics of corporation stock is its alienability.

However, corporations may impose reasonable restraints on transfer, aimed at promoting corporate objectives. In fact, the close-corporation statutes of Delaware, Illinois, Kansas, Maryland, Pennsylvania, and Wisconsin *require* the imposition of transfer restrictions.

Almost half the states (see the statute table on pages 110–111 for cites) have provisions dealing with transfer restrictions in general. These statutes, which are quite similar, state that corporations may impose reasonable transfer restrictions such as:

- a requirement that a would-be seller offer the shares to the corporation or to the other shareholders before selling them outside
- a ban on transfers that would disqualify the corporation as an S corporation
- designating classes of acceptable transferees (e.g., spouses, immediate family, other shareholders) or unacceptable transferees (e.g., competitors). Sometimes a distinction is drawn between transfers to members of the transferor's immediate family and to outsiders; some restrictions apply to sales but not to transfers by will or in trust.

Transfer restrictions can be imposed in the Articles of Incorporation or by-laws. Many states also provide that the restrictions can be imposed by agreement of the shareholders—but sometimes the statutes provide that such an agreement will not be binding on shareholders who are not signatories to the agreement. Several state statutes make the sensible requirement that the transfer restrictions be endorsed on the share certificate. This is good policy in any case. Under the UCC, a third party isn't bound by a transfer restriction unless he/she has actual notice of it—[see *Norman v. Jeuch Corp.*, 501 P.2d 305 (Oregon 1972); *Ling & Co. v. Trinity Savings & Loan Ass'n*, 482 SW2d 841 (Texas 1972); *Irwin v. West End Development Co.*, 481 F.2d 34 (10th Cir. 1973).] What better way to give actual notice than to put the restriction on the face of the certificate?

The provision or agreement establishing the transfer restrictions must also set a mechanism for pricing the stock that will be transferred. The possibilities include:

- mutual agreement at the time of the transfer
- book value at the time of transfer
- capitalized earnings over the pre-transfer period

- value of comparable shares
- best bona fide offer from an outsider
- arbitration

It must also be clear as to whether all of the other shareholders or only certain shareholders have a right to buy the stock, what happens if several shareholders want the same stock, and whether original ownership percentages are to be preserved. Shareholders covered by such provisions or agreements must arrange their personal finances so that liquidity will be available if they want to buy stock offered to them; many close-corporation shareholders have a high net worth, but few cash assets, and find themselves unable to take advantage of an attractive offer.

Voting Trusts and Voting Agreements

All of the states permit voting trusts (usually with a limitation of ten-year trust terms, generally renewable); some of them make additional provisions for voting agreements, either with the same ten-year limitation or without limitations on duration. The purpose of either device is to weld shareholders who would individually have little voting power into a powerful majority or plurality voting bloc.

EXAMPLE: East End Automotive Service, Inc. has eight shareholders—one holding 25%, one holding 20%, five with 10% each, and the last shareholder with a mere 5%—only the 25% and 20% shareholder can anticipate much of a voice in corporate affairs. (But note that, even acting together, they can't get a clear majority—they need the cooperation of at least one other shareholder.) However, if the six smaller shareholders form a trust or agreement, they'll control the corporation.

To create a voting trust, the participating shareholders sign an agreement setting out the trust's terms; then they actually transfer their shares to the trustee, who then becomes eligible to vote the shares. Depending on state law, it may be necessary to file the trust agreement or a statement of the shareholders and shares bound by it with the corporation, and for the document to be available for inspection by shareholders. Remember that the provisions of Subchapter S allow a voting trust to be an S corporation stockholder, so the use of this device will not terminate the S corporation election. The owners of the stock remain beneficial owners, and they, not the trustee, get the dividends. Sometimes the agreement provides that the trustee will issue transferrable voting trust certificates so that, in effect, the stockholders can sell their shares.

A voting agreement is an agreement among a number of shareholders, providing that they will vote together, either in all circumstances under which they are permitted to vote or only in certain circumstances (e.g., ratification of mergers or acquisitions). ***PRACTICE TIP:*** *In some states, a voting agreement has the advantage of a permissible duration as long as the stockholders want it; other states restrict the agreement to a ten-year or other limited term.*

The practical distinction is that a voting trust makes it much harder for a stockholder to renege: his or her shares have already been transferred, and the trustee is quite unlikely to vote other than as instructed. Voting agreements are specifically enforceable, but a suit for violation of the agreement is a classic instance of locking the barn door after the horse is gone.

Other Shareholder Agreements

Corporations—especially those covered by state close corporation statutes—can also be governed by shareholder agreements. In general, all the shareholders must agree for the agreements to be binding on the corporation and those who do business with it. State law may require the agreement to be entered in the corporation's minutes.

Ohio (at §1701.59.1) has a particularly comprehensive statute dealing with shareholder agreements. Such agreements may deal with:

- management of corporate business
- shareholders' right to dissolve the corporation on deadlock
- super-majority requirements
- permission for one person to hold multiple corporate offices (in effect, to reduce the size of the group of officers)
- terms and conditions under which employees and officers serve (e.g., power to remove them)
- dividend policy (shareholders who will not be employed by the corporation may want the corporation to commit to paying dividends and to require a certain level of payment based on certain profit levels)
- elimination of the Board of Directors in favor of management by all the shareholders
- additional rights to inspect corporate books and records
- limitations on, or prohibition of, issuance of additional shares
- mandatory arbitration in case of deadlock

Such agreements are specifically enforceable. *PRACTICE TIP: If you're representing minority shareholders, the time to press for such an agreement is in the pre-incorporation period (when the business founders need their money), and before internal stresses have had a chance to develop.*

Preemptive Rights

It is common for corporations to authorize (via the Articles of Incorporation) the issuance of far more shares than they intend to issue during the start-up period. That way, the shares can be issued and sold later, when an infusion of capital is needed.

However, these shares could easily become tools in a pattern of oppression of minority shareholders by the majority. All that would have to be done would be to issue a flood of shares at a time when the minority holders are cash-poor. Then the majority shareholders can buy up the shares or sell them to friends who can be counted upon for their votes.

Therefore, all the states have provisions dealing with preemptive rights. Preemptive rights mean that stockholders have a right to acquire newly issued shares in quantities that will preserve their original percentage ownership. (As to whether they'll be able to afford the shares ... that's another question.)

The state laws come in two varieties. In the majority of these laws, preemptive rights exist unless the Articles of Incorporation limit or deny them. However, the general rule is that preemptive rights do not exist in shares issued for noncash consideration, or in shares issued as incentive benefits for employees and officers.

In the minority jurisdictions (Arizona, California, Delaware, Florida, Indiana, Kansas, Louisiana, Maryland, Massachusetts, Mississippi, Montana, New Jersey, Oklahoma, Pennsylvania, Vermont, and West Virginia), preemptive rights exist only to the extent permitted in the Articles of Incorporation.

PRACTICE TIP: Therefore, the lawyer handling a business start-up must become familiar with the state statute; must determine his or her clients' wishes; and must make sure that the Articles of Incorporation provide preemptive rights (if mandated), or limit the preemptive rights as desired.

Cumulative Voting

The usual rule in corporate democracy is one vote per share (although most states permit variations in voting rights imposed by Articles of Incorporation or bylaws). The most prominent exception is cumulative voting. That is, when the shareholders are electing the Board of Directors, they are permitting a total number of votes equalling the number of shares they hold times the number of directors to be elected. Then he or she may divide the votes as he or she likes. For example, if five directors are to be elected, and the stockholder owns 500 shares, he or she has 2,500 votes and may give all or part of them to a single candidate.

The effect of cumulative voting is to make it easier for minority shareholders to elect directors by concentrating their votes on single or a few candidates.

In 14 states, cumulative voting is mandatory in all elections for directors. This is the case in Arizona, Arkansas, Kansas, Kentucky, Mississippi, Missouri, Montana, Nebraska, New Jersey, North Dakota, Ohio, South Dakota, West Virginia, and Wyoming.

In the other 35 states (Massachusetts has no provisions about cumulative voting), the more common approach is to say that cumulative voting is permitted only if the Articles of Incorporation so specify. This is true of Alabama, California, Connecticut, Delaware, the District of Columbia, Florida, Georgia, Indiana, Iowa, Louisiana, Maine, Maryland, Michigan, Nevada, New Hampshire, New Mexico, New York, Oklahoma, Oregon, Rhode Island, Tennessee, Vermont, Virginia, and Wisconsin.

The third group of jurisdictions (Alaska, Colorado, Hawaii, Idaho, Illinois, Minnesota, North Carolina, Pennsylvania, South Carolina, Texas, Utah, and Washington) assumes cumulative voting as a "default option": that is, it exists unless limited or denied by the Articles of Incorporation.

A number of states (California, Connecticut, Hawaii, Nevada, Ohio, Wisconsin) require either that voters who intend to cumulate their votes give notice before the meeting, or that *someone* must give such notice before cumulative voting will be allowed.

PRACTICE TIP: *Thus, the interview and drafting processes must include consideration of cumulative voting, and the drafter must make sure that the necessary provisions to permit or limit cumulative voting, as desired and in conformity with state law, must be included in the Articles of Incorporation.*

Super-Majority

It's a bird, it's a plane ... no, it's not a mild-mannered stockholder who turns into an avenger, but a provision in the Articles of Incorporation requiring more than a majority of shareholder votes for certain actions. One common context in which the super-majority provision is used is the sale of substantial amounts of corporate assets or mergers and acquisitions: to prevent squeeze-outs by the majority, the minority can press for provisions that, in effect, give them veto power.

The super-majority provision is a fairly popular one in state corporation codes [see Arizona §10-143; Colorado §7-4-118; Connecticut §33-329; Iowa §496A.138; Kentucky §271A.655; Michigan §450.1455; Nebraska §21-20,128; New Hampshire §293-A:149; New Jersey §14A:5-12; New Mexico §53-18-6; North Carolina §55-56; Oklahoma Title 18 §1.56; Oregon §57.586; Rhode Island §7-1.1-30.1; Tennessee §48-1-711; Vermont Title 11 §2210, and Wyoming §17-1-1004.]

Deadlock

The worst thing that can happen to a closely held corporation's balance of power is deadlock: the stockholders have formed blocs that are dedicated to spiking the guns of the other blocs. The end result is that the corporation can't make any decisions because the various factions have veto power.

Various state corporation codes have deadlock provisions, permitting dissatisfied shareholders to be bought out. That way, at least they can receive some value for their investment in the corporation. If the corporation is incorporated in a state that lacks such provisions, or if this appraisal right is limited to dissenters in merger situations, consider adding a provision to the Articles of Incorporation or bylaws dealing with deadlock. One common provision gives a buy-out formula for the shareholders opposed to corporate policy; another possibility is to require all the shareholders to submit to binding arbitration, and either to take action based on the arbitration (ending the deadlock) or to accept a buy-out. Depending on state law and the corporation's charter, dissenting stockholders may even have a "doomsday device": they may have the power to dissolve the corporation if deadlock persists, or a court may have the power to dissolve the corporation on petition of a stockholder.

If this is a possibility in the jurisdiction of incorporation, be sure that the Articles of Incorporation and/or bylaws come to grips with this situation, and detail what will happen to the corporation's assets, contracts, and receivables if the corporation is dissolved.

Summary

It is a serious mistake for drafters to treat the Articles of Incorporation as boring hunks of boilerplate. The provisions of the Articles of Incorporation, and of the bylaws and any agreements of the stockholders between themselves or involving the corporation, have a tremendous effect on corporate structure, governance, and the balance of power among shareholders.

Forms

ARTICLES OF INCORPORATION FOR A CLOSE CORPORATION

1. The corporation will be known as _____ . This corporate name has already been reserved/if this corporate name is unavailable, the corporation will be known as _____ .

2. The corporation will be incorporated in the state of _____ , although it may do business in other states and countries.

3. The corporation is to be incorporated as a [statutory] close corporation, as described in §§ _____ of the laws of the state of _____ . To this end, it will not have more than _____ shareholders until and unless it chooses to waive the election of close-corporation status.

4. The corporation intends to elect Subchapter S status.

5. The corporation's duration will be perpetual/a term of _____ years from incorporation.

6. The corporation is formed for legally permitted purposes, including but not limited to: _____ . However, at no time will the corporation provide banking or insurance services, or hold itself out as providing such services.

7. The corporation's initial registered agent is _____ : the corporation's initial registered address is _____ .

8. The names and addresses of the corporation's incorporators are: _____ .

9. The corporation will be governed directly by its stockholders as long as it does business as a close corporation; there will be no Board of Directors. *OR* The corporation's initial Board of Directors, who will serve until the organization meeting, are: _____ .

10. The corporation is authorized to issue shares as follows:
_____ shares of no-par common stock/common stock with a par value of $ _____ per share.
_____ shares of no-par preferred stock/preferred stock with a par value of $ _____ per share, and with rights and preference described as follows: _____ .

11. However, as long as the corporation has a valid Subchapter S election, no stock will actually be issued other than one class of common stock. However, although all such shares of common stock will have identical rights in the corporation's assets, they may differ as to voting rights.

12. Preemptive rights will not be granted/preemptive rights will be granted as follows: _____ .

13. All shares of the corporation's stock issued at a time when the corporation is a close corporation will be subject to the following transfer restrictions: _____ .

14. A meeting of shareholders will be held, either inside or outside the state of incorporation, at least once a year. [If there is a Board of Directors, add:] A meeting of directors will be held, either inside or outside the state of incorporation, at least once a year. Meetings may be held by conference

telephone call as well as in person. Any action that could be taken by a shareholders' or directors' meeting can be taken without a meeting on unanimous consent of all persons qualified to vote.

15. The corporation's officers will be a President, Vice-President, Secretary, and Treasurer. The officers will be appointed by the stockholders/the Board of Directors. Any person may hold any combination of offices.

Signed: _____ [Incorporator(s)]

Date: _____

Notariat: _____

NOTE: Be sure to comply with any publication requirement imposed by the state of incorporation.

PARTNERSHIP AGREEMENT

1. This agreement is made on the _____ day of _____ , 19 _____
between _____ , _____ , and
_____ who wish to form a partnership, to be known as
_____ .

2. The partnership will engage in lawful business, including but not
limited to: _____ .

3. The partnership's duration will be until _____ , 19 _____/until the
partnership terminates under the laws of _____ /until the
partnership terminates by mutual consent of all persons who are then
partners.

4. The partners have contributed capital to the partnership as follows:

Partner's Name	Cash	Property (describe + FMV)

5. Partners may be required to contribute additional capital to the
partnership under the following circumstances: _____ .

6. Each partner agrees to devote his/her best efforts to partnership
business [and agrees to work full time for the business], and to refrain
from competing with the partnership or appropriating partnership
opportunities.

7. Each partner is entitled to a weekly/monthly "draw" against his/her
share of partnership profits, as follows:
Partner A:
Partner B:
Partner C: (etc.)

8. Partners are entitled to share in partnership profits in the following
percentages:
Partner A:
Partner B:
Partner C:

9. Partners are entitled to a pass-through of partnership losses in the
following percentages, which will be used in preparing the partnership's
federal income tax information return:
Partner A:
Partner B:
Partner C:
All partners agree that they will abide by the allocation of loss items as
provided by the partnership's federal income tax information return.
_____ is hereby designated as the tax management partner
for purposes of any partnership-level audit carried out by the IRS.

10. All partners have entered into a buy-sell agreement, the terms of
which are hereby incorporated by reference. Each partner agrees to buy
and maintain a life insurance and disability insurance policy on each of
the other partners, in an amount at least equal to $ _____ .

11. All partners agree that the partnership may continue to do business and will not be terminated by events (e.g., death of a partner) that would work technical dissolution of the partnership.

12. A partner may transfer his or her partnership interest at any time, for any sum of money or amount of property, provided that he/she receives advance permission for the transfer and succession of the transferee to the original partner's interest, from all other partners. The successor partner will have all the rights and liabilities of the original partner, and must subscribe to the buy-sell agreement on the same terms as the original partner.

13. All partners agree to the establishment of a defined-benefit/defined-contribution Keogh plan for the partnership.

Signatures of Partners: _____, _____,
_____

VOTING AGREEMENT

1. This agreement is signed on the _____ day of _____, 19 ____ between _____ minority shareholders of _____ Corporation.

2. The names and shareholdings of the signers are as follows:

Name   # of common shares owned   % of total common shares owned

3. The signers are making this agreement because they want to vote together in order to have a significant influence on the composition of the Board of Directors of _____ Corporation.

4. Therefore, the signers agree that they will, as long as this agreement is in force, vote all their shares (whether owned at the time of signing, or later acquired by purchase or by exercise of preemptive rights) as a bloc in all elections for directors of _____ Corporation. Although the signers may vote as a bloc on other decisions submitted to the stockholders, they are not obliged to do so.

5. At least ____ days before each annual meeting, the signers will meet and take a written vote on the way the bloc of votes will be cast and, if state law and the corporation's charter permit, whether the right of cumulative voting will be exercised. Decisions on voting will be made by the vote of the majority of shares covered by this agreement.

6. As required by § ____ of the laws of the state of _____ , this agreement will be filed at the main office of _____ Corporation, which is located at _____ .

7. This agreement binds and benefits the signers, their heirs, personal representatives, and assigns.

8. Although the laws of the state of _____ do not place a limitation on the term of voting agreements, the signers agree that the term of this agreement will be limited to ____ years, unless terminated sooner under Paragraph 9, below.
OR   This agreement will continue as long as _____ Corporation is in existence, or until it is terminated under Paragraph 9, below.
OR   As required by § ____ of the laws of the state of _____ the term of this agreement will be ____ years, unless terminated sooner under Paragraph 9, below.

9. Any signer may call a meeting of signers at any time, for the purpose of voting on the termination of this agreement. The agreement will be terminated if the owners of ____ % or more of the shares covered by this agreement give their written consent to termination. If the agreement is terminated, the Corporation will be notified, and it will no longer be required that the existence and effect of this voting agreement be endorsed on share certificates.

10. The signers will use their best efforts to induce _____ Corporation to place a sticker on all common stock certificates (whether already issued or to be issued in the future) indicating the existence of this agreement and its potential effects on corporate elections.

Signed,

SHAREHOLDER AGREEMENT DEALING
WITH TRANSFER RESTRICTIONS

1. _____ Corporation, incorporated in the state of
_____, is capitalized as follows: _____ shares common, _____
shares preferred.

2. The stock is held as follows:

Shareholder's name   Common   Preferred
                       # of shares/ % total   # of shares/ % total

3. This agreement, which is unanimously subscribed to by all
shareholders, places restrictions on the transfer of ☐ all shares of
_____ Corporation stock
☐ all common shares
☐ all preferred shares.

4. Restrictions apply to:
☐ all voluntary transfers, and transfers incident to marital property
settlements
☐ sales and exchanges only
☐ sales and exchanges involving any person other than a signer of this
agreement or a member of a signing shareholder's own immediate family
☐ sales and exchanges involving more than _____ % of
_____ Corporation's common/preferred stock outstanding at
the time of the sale or exchange
☐ dispositions by will or in trust.

5. The signers agree that they will not impair _____
Corporation's status as an S corporation, and will perform any reasonable
action needed to maintain such status on request by the corporation or
fellow shareholders.

6. The signers agree that, as to all shares and transactions covered by this
agreement:
• they will notify the Corporation's secretary of their intent to transfer
shares, within _____ days of the decision to attempt a transfer
• they will not transfer the shares unless every person entitled to exercise
an option to purchase has declined to exercise the option.

7. _____ Corporation will have a first option to acquire the
shares; if the corporation declines to exercise its option or if sufficient
funds are unavailable, the other stockholders will have a second option in
any shares a stockholder wants to transfer, and which have not been
optioned by the corporation.

8. The stockholders will be able to exercise their individual second
options:
☐ on any terms which they can negotiate with the stockholder who wants
to transfer shares
☐ in a proportion equal to their percentage ownership before the transfer.
Unless all the other stockholders exercise this right, the option will lapse.
☐ with priority according to their existing holdings; that is, the stockholder
with the largest holding has first choice of shares available for option,
followed by the other stockholders in order of holdings. However, no

stockholder may buy shares increasing his or her proportion of ownership by more than _____ %.

9. All optioned shares may be paid for in cash; in marketable securities of other corporations; or, if the selling shareholder agrees, by promissory notes on terms acceptable to the selling shareholder.

10. The price for the shares subject to option shall be:
☐ negotiated between the selling shareholder and the corporation or purchasing shareholders
☐ equal to the book value of the shares at the time the intention to transfer is announced
☐ the current value of the shares as determined by the buy-sell agreement signed by all the shareholders on _____ , 19 ____
☐ equal to the highest bona fide offer the selling shareholder has had from a prospective buyer other than the corporation or the other shareholders
☐ the price set by a qualified appraiser, with the appraiser's fee to be borne by ☐ the corporation ☐ the selling shareholder ☐ the party or parties offering to purchase shares subject to option ☐ all the shareholders, in proportion to their stock ownership before the announcement of the intended transfer.

11. Any shares that are not optioned either by the corporation or by the other shareholders may be transferred freely, with the proviso that all shareholders agree not to transfer any shares to a competitor of the corporation, or to any controlling shareholder of a competitor of the corporation.

12. Shares may be transferred freely, without the need to resort to the option procedure, if the selling shareholder has obtained a written waiver of option from the corporation's Secretary and from each of the other shareholders.

13. If any signing shareholder is also an employee of the corporation, and if at any time he/she resigns, retires, or is discharged by the corporation, all of his or her shares will immediately become subject to option, as described in this agreement.

14. The signing shareholders agree to attach a sticker describing these transfer restrictions to all their share certificates evidencing ownership of the corporation's stock.

15. This agreement represents the entire agreement among the shareholders dealing with share transfer restrictions. This agreement benefits and burdens the shareholders themselves, their heirs, and assigns. This agreement may not be altered or modified orally, and may be altered in writing only with consent of all signers.

16. Any provision of this agreement that is found unconscionable or unenforceable by any court at any time will be severed, and the rest of the agreement will continue in force and effect.

Date:

Signatures:

VOTING TRUST AGREEMENT

1. The signing stockholders, and any other stockholders who later join them in this agreement, want to create a voting trust so that they can influence the policy of _____ Corporation by having all their stock voted by a trustee. The trust begins on the date of signing, given below, and continues for a term of _____ years—but not longer than the _____ -year term permitted by § _____ of the laws of the State of _____ .

2. At all times this voting trust is in effect, there will be _____ Trustee(s). _____ has/have agreed to serve as the initial Trustee(s).

3. If any Trustee dies, resigns, or is removed, all the signing stockholders will meet within _____ days of the event and will elect a successor Trustee by majority vote.

4. The Trustee(s) agree(s) to hold the shares of stock transferred to the trust by the signing shareholders, and to vote the shares in accordance with the terms of this agreement. When all the signing shareholders (and any shareholders who later join in the agreement) have endorsed the certificates of all their voting shares in _____ Corporation in blank and delivered them to the Trustee(s), the Trustee(s) will surrender the certificates to the proper officer of _____ Corporation. The corporate officer will then cancel the certificates and issue new certificates to the Trustee(s).

5. The Trustee(s) will issue each signing shareholder a trust certificate for the number of shares surrendered. A trust certificate can be assigned as if it were a stock certificate; however, the Trustee(s) rather than the corporation's secretary/transfer agent must be notified of the assignment. On notice to the Trustee(s), the transferee will assume all the rights of the transferor.

6. The Trustee(s) is/are authorized to represent the signers and to vote all their shares at all regular and special meetings, dealing with all ordinary and extraordinary corporate transactions.

7. The Trustee(s) shall vote the shares as a bloc,
☐ according to his/her/its best judgment
☐ by majority vote of the Trustees
☐ in accordance with instructions provided by the signing shareholders, after a special meeting held not more than _____ days or less than _____ days before the corporate meeting at which the shares are to be voted.

8. All dividends on shares covered by this agreement will be paid to the Trustee(s). Dividends will be applied first to the Trustee(s)' expenses of serving as Trustee(s); next to trustee compensation, as follows: _____ . All remaining dividends will be remitted to the signing shareholders in proportion to the number of shares surrendered under this agreement. If the dividends are smaller than the total expenses and commissions, the signing shareholders agree to contribute to the deficiency, in proportion to the number of shares surrendered under this

agreement. The Trustee(s) will notify them of the shortfall, and of their proportionate share; the signing shareholders will pay their share of the shortfall by personal check to each Trustee, within _____ days of receiving the notice.

9. The signing shareholders as a class agree to indemnify the Trustee(s) against any loss, damage, or liability sustained while faithfully carrying out the terms of the agreement. The indemnity obligation will be distributed proportional to the number of shares surrendered.

Date:

Signed,

Name   Signature   # of Voting Shares Held   % of Total Voting Shares

TRANSFER RESTRICTION ENDORSEMENT
FOR STOCK CERTIFICATES

☐ These shares are subject to transfer restrictions as adopted by a resolution of the stockholders/directors of the _____ Corporation, passed at the meeting of _____ , 19 ____ and expressed in the minutes of that meeting.

☐ These shares are subject to restrictions created by unanimous agreement of all persons who owned stock on _____ 19 ____ , the date of the agreement. Copies of the agreement are on file at the Secretary's office, located at: _____ .

☐ These shares are subject to the Corporation's right of first refusal to purchase the shares at $ _____ a share/the net asset value of the shares.

☐ THESE SECURITIES HAVE NOT BEEN REGISTERED UNDER THE SECURITIES ACT OF 1933, AND MAY NOT BE OFFERED, OFFERED FOR SALE, OR SOLD IN THE ABSENCE OF AN EFFECTIVE REGISTRATION STATEMENT UNDER THE SECURITIES ACT OR ANY OPINION OF COUNSEL SATISFACTORY TO THE CORPORATION THAT REGISTRATION IS NOT REQUIRED.

SAMPLE BYLAWS

General Provisions

1. The corporation's name will be _____. (OR: The corporation's registered name will be _____; it will do business under the artificial name of _____.)

2. The corporation's registered address will be: _____.

3. The corporation's registered agent for the service of process at its registered address will be: _____.

4. The corporation will have a calendar year / a fiscal year beginning on _____ and ending on _____.

5. The corporation will adopt a seal, described as follows:

_____.

Bylaws Dealing With Stock

1. Shares of the corporation's stock will be deemed fully paid and nonassessable when adequate consideration has been received for them. Adequate consideration can include money, tangible or intangible property, and/or services that have actually been performed for the corporation. However, neither promissory notes nor future services will be acceptable as consideration. Absent fraud, the Board of Directors' decision as to the adequacy of consideration will be final. The use of consideration for the sale of stock to defray the expenses of organizing the corporation will not impair the stock's characterization as fully paid and nonassessable.

2. All stockholders will receive certificates, signed by the corporation's President and Secretary, and bearing the corporation's seal, evidencing their ownership of shares.

3. All share certificates will be endorsed with transfer restrictions as follows: _____, either printed on the certificate or attached in the form of a sticker.

4. Lost, stolen, or destroyed certificates can be replaced if the shareholder of record gives the corporation an affidavit that the certificates have been lost, stolen, or destroyed; and if the shareholder of record posts bond indemnifying the corporation against claims arising out of the loss, etc. However, the corporation will not follow this procedure unless it has been notified before it is notified of the acquisition of the certificates by a bona fide purchaser who did not have notice of any adverse claim.

5. The corporation will register stock transfers on its books if the intended transferor pays all applicable stock-transfer taxes; the certificates for the shares to be transferred are properly endorsed by the holder of record or his or her authorized representative; and if the endorsement is witnessed by ____ witnesses (unless the corporation's Secretary has agreed to

waive this requirement). The corporation will not register a transfer if it has notice of adverse claims, but it has no duty to inquire as to the possibility of adverse claims.

Meetings of Shareholders

1. The annual meeting to elect directors and carry out other corporate business will be held on the ____ day of _____ of each year. If this date is not a business day, the meeting will be held on the next business day.

2. In addition to the annual meeting, special meetings may be called by the President, by resolution of the Board of Directors, or at the instance of shareholders whose combined shareholdings are equal to or greater than ____ % of the corporation's outstanding voting stock.

3. The normal location for both regular and special meetings will be the corporation's headquarters, located at _____, but a meeting may legally be held at any place either inside or outside the state of original incorporation.

4. The corporation's Secretary will compile and maintain a list of shareholders of record entitled to vote. The list will be available at the corporation's headquarters, for inspection by shareholders and their authorized representatives, at any time during normal business hours. This list will be amended from time to time, based on transfers disclosed as provided above.

5. Notice will be sent, by first-class mail, to every shareholder entitled to vote (that is, every holder of record of voting stock, as evidenced by the company's books ____ days before a meeting). Notice will be sent not less than 10 and not more than 30 days before a meeting. All notices will give the date, time, and location of the meeting; all notices of special meetings will also give the purpose for which the meeting is called.

6. Notice of meeting may be waived in writing by any shareholder. A shareholder's attendance at a meeting, in person or by proxy, will be construed as waiver of notice.

7. Shareholders can vote either by appearing at a meeting or by submitting a written proxy to the corporation's Secretary not more than 30 days before a meeting.

8. The quorum for a shareholder's meeting consists of a majority of the voting shares, represented either in person or by proxy. If there is a quorum at a meeting, the meeting may legally continue and take action even if some of the shareholders leave before the end of the meeting, even if the departure brings the number of shares represented below the quorum level.

9. On all matters other than election of directors, the rule will be "one share–one vote." However, cumulative voting for directors will be permitted. That is, each shareholder will have as many votes as the number of his or her shares times the number of directors to be elected; the shareholder may apportion these votes among the candidates in any way he or she chooses.

10. The agenda for the annual meeting shall be:
   A. Meeting called to order
   B. Presentation of proxies
   C. Determination of quorum
   D. Reading and approval of minutes of previous meetings
   E. Officers' reports
   F. Election of directors
   G. Any other business before the meeting.

The corporation's President will preside at the annual meeting.

11. Any action that could be taken at a shareholders' meeting may be taken without a meeting on unanimous written consent of all stockholders eligible to vote.

12. These bylaws may be amended by majority vote of the shareholders entitled to vote.

The Board of Directors

1. The corporation will be managed by its Board of Directors. The powers of the Board include the power to:
   A. authorize loans to the corporation by passing a resolution
   B. determine signature requirements for the corporation's checks
   C. determine if dividends will be paid in a given quarter; if so, to set the dividend level and determine whether the dividends will be paid in cash, property, or stock
   D. amend these bylaws.

2. The Board will consist of five directors, who need not be shareholders of the corporation or residents of the state of the corporation's original incorporation.

3. The initial directors, named in the corporation's Articles of Incorporation, will serve until the corporation's first annual meeting, at which time five directors will be elected.

4. The regular annual meeting of the Board of Directors will be held each year immediately after the shareholders' meeting, and in the same place. Regular quarterly meetings will be held three, six, and nine months after the annual meeting, in the same place. This bylaw constitutes notice of the four regular meetings of each year.

5. Special meetings can be called at any time, by the corporation's President or by any two directors. Special meetings may be held at any place inside or outside the state of original incorporation. Directors must be notified of special meetings by telegram, at least two days before the meeting, unless they have waived notice of meeting; appearance at a meeting constitutes waiver of notice. Valid meetings may also be held by conference telephone call or video teleconferencing.

6. The quorum for any Board of Directors meeting shall be three.

7. If a quorum is present at a meeting, the act of the majority of the directors present constitutes the act of the Board of Directors.

8. Any action that could be taken by a directors' meeting can be taken without a meeting on unanimous written consent of all the directors.

9. Directors present at Board meetings are presumed to assent in all actions taken at the meeting if they voted for the action, or unless they both caused a dissent to be entered in the minutes of the meeting and filed a written dissent with the corporation's Secretary within _____ days of the meeting.

10. Directors will be compensated $ _____ for each meeting they attend, but will not receive any expense reimbursement for such meetings.

Officers

1. The Board of Directors will appoint the corporation's officers, to serve for a one-year term. The Board of Directors will also set the salary and other compensation to be paid to the officers.

2. The corporation's officers will be a President, Vice-President, Secretary, and Treasurer. The same person may not be both President and Secretary; any person may hold any other combination of offices. A director may serve as an officer of the corporation, but may not vote on his or her own tenure or compensation.

3. The Board of Directors will hold a special meeting and appoint a successor whenever any officer dies, retires, or is removed from office. The successor will serve until the next annual directors' meeting.

4. Officers may be removed from office when, in the judgment of the Board of Directors, they are not acting in the best interests of the corporation. If the person removed from office has an employment contract, the remedies provided by the contract shall be exclusive.

5. The President will be the corporation's chief executive officer. The President will have day-to-day responsibility for managing corporate affairs; will preside at shareholders' and directors' meetings; and will sign the corporation's stock certificates and other corporate documents as authorized by the Board of Directors.

6. The Vice-President will perform the President's duties if he/she is absent, unable to act, or has been removed. If the President also serves as Vice-President, the Board will appoint a person to serve as Vice-President, either temporarily or until the next annual directors' meeting, when any of these events occur.

7. The Secretary's duties include keeping the minutes of shareholders' and directors' meetings, and entering the minutes in the corporation's official minutes book; issuing notices as required by state law or the corporation's Articles of Incorporation or bylaws; maintaining custody of the corporate records and corporate seal; affixing the corporate seal to documents to evidence official corporate actions; maintaining a list of stockholders and stockholders entitled to vote; updating the list in light of stock transfers; and signing stock certificates.

8. The Treasurer will be the corporation's chief financial officer, and will be responsible for custody of the corporate funds and securities, maintaining records of corporate income and expenses, and performing

cash management tasks to secure the highest income compatible with safety for corporate funds not otherwise employed.

Indemnification

1. The corporation agrees to indemnify its officers and directors against all civil and criminal liability incurred while acting prudently as officers and directors, carrying out the policies of the corporation or taking actions which they, in good faith, believed were in the best interests of the corporation. Officers and directors are also entitled to indemnification for reliance in good faith on professional advice, or on facts supplied by a person who could reasonably be expected to possess accurate information.

2. Indemnification extends to the costs of litigation as well as judgments rendered against the officer or director and settlements of claims against the officer or director.

3. The Treasurer shall have discretion to decide whether the corporation should maintain liability insurance policies for its directors and officers, or whether the corporation should be a self-insurer for this purpose; and also to determine the size of reserves that should be maintained against the possibility that indemnification will be required.

Interested Officer and Director Transactions

1. Transactions between the corporation and other organizations in which an officer or director is involved will be valid, and will be neither void nor voidable, if the contract (measured as of the time of signing) was fair to the corporation, and the interested party disclosed his or her interest in good faith, and obtained the approval of a majority of the noninterested directors and/or ratification by a majority of the holders of voting stock.

Majority-Minority Shareholder Relations

1. Any shareholder, or any person designated by a signed writing as the representative of a shareholder, shall have the right to inspect the company's books and records at any time during normal business hours, without the necessity of giving advance notice.

2. Any merger, acquisition, sale of a division of the corporation, reorganization or recapitalization of the corporation, or bulk sale of more than ____ % of the corporation's inventory or assets will require the advance consent of shareholders holding ____ % or more of the corporation's outstanding voting stock.

3. Shareholders will have preemptive rights in all stock authorized by the Articles of Incorporation but issued after the corporation's start-up period. However, preemptive rights will not apply to stock issued to the corporation's employees, officers, or directors as part of their compensation or as a bonus or incentive.

ARTICLES OF INCORPORATION FOR A PROFESSIONAL CORPORATION

1. This agreement is made on the _____ day of _____, 19 _____ between _____, _____, _____, and _____, all of whom are over 21 and are licensed to practice the profession of _____ in the state of _____. They make this agreement because they wish to practice the profession of _____ together, in the form of a professional corporation/professional association.

2. The professional practice will be known as _____ PC/PA; this name will be used on all of the practice's public communications, including letterheads, bill forms, invoices, and brochures.

3. If the practice already exists in partnership form, all of the practice's clients and creditors will be notified of the change of form of operation within _____ days of the adoption of this agreement.

4. The purpose of the corporation/association is to practice the profession of _____ ; to buy, lease, hold, mortgage, lend, borrow, pledge, and use real and personal property and money, to that end. The corporation/association shall be empowered to offer its services to the public and to institutions; to participate in prepaid professional services plans; to hire professionals and support staff as common-law employees; to purchase and maintain liability insurance policies and/or carry out a program of self-insurance; and to perform other actions permitted to professional corporations/associations by the laws of the state of _____.

5. The corporation/association's duration will be perpetual/a term of _____ years/until the death or retirement from professional practice of the last signatory or professional later admitted to membership in the corporation/association.

6. The corporation/association's principal office will be located at _____ in the City and County of _____.

7. The corporation's registered agent for the service of process at that address will be _____.

8. The corporation is authorized to issue _____ shares of voting common stock, _____ shares of nonvoting common stock, and _____ shares of perferred stock, described as follows as to class, series, par value, preferences, and rights: _____. At no time may any stock be issued to any person who is not licensed to practice the profession of _____ in the state of _____; nor may a stockholder transfer any stock, whether inter vivos or by will, to any person other than a licensed professional.

9. The initial shareholders in the corporation/association will be the signatories. They will receive stock, in return for consideration, as follows:

Name   # and type of shares   Consideration provided

10. The signatories will act as incorporators of the professional corporation/association. Their addresses are:

Name   Address

11. The corporation/association will not commence to practice the profession in corporate/association form until it has received $_____ as consideration for the issuance of shares.

12. The signatories will serve as the corporation's/association's Board of Directors until the initial meeting of the shareholders/incorporators/initial directors, to be held _____, 19____. The first regular Board of Directors will be elected at this meeting, to serve until the next annual meeting.

13. The corporation/association may, at any time, hire persons licensed to practice the profession of _____ as common-law employees, who will not be stockholders or have the rights or obligations of stockholders. However, the corporation/association will never, at any time, permit professional services to be rendered by any person other than a licensed professional. All paraprofessionals will be supervised at all times by a licensed professional.

14. The corporation/association may, at any time, admit further licensed professionals to stockholder status, on consent of all existing stockholders, and on payment of consideration to be set by the existing stockholders.

15. All stockholders will be jointly and severally liable for all negligence, malpractice, wrongful acts, and acts and omissions of all the stockholders and all persons directly supervised by stockholders, if the negligence or other act complained of occurred in connection with the rendering of professionals services by the corporation/association and/or its stockholders.

PRE-INCORPORATION AGREEMENT WITH PROMOTER

1. _____, _____, and _____ are the incorporators of a business to be known as _____. They contemplate incorporation in the state of _____, for the purpose of carrying out business activities including but not limited to _____. (In this agreement, they will be known as the *incorporators*.)

2. _____, to be known as the *promoter* is experienced in the promotion of the stock of new corporations, and has the following licenses: _____.

3. The incorporators and the promoter enter into this agreement so that the promoter can use his experience in the promotion and sale of corporate stock to obtain subscriptions for, and to sell, stock in the corporation to be formed by the incorporators.

4. The incorporators contemplate that the corporation will be authorized to issue stock as follows:

Type	Number of Shares	Par Value (or No-Par)

5. The incorporators propose an initial offering of ____ shares of common stock at an estimated offering price of $ _____ per share, and ____ shares of preferred stock at an estimated offering price of $ _____ per share, to be sold in the state(s) of: _____. It is contemplated that this issue will be:
☐ public
☐ intrastate only
☐ in compliance with Regulation A
☐ in compliance with Regulation D

6. The incorporators will use their best efforts to incorporate in the state of _____ and carry out any applicable requirements of the Securities Act, Securities Exchange Act, and the Blue Sky Laws of the state(s) of _____.

7. The incorporators will give the promoter full information about the progress of the offering, and will promptly provide the promoter with at least ____ copies of the required disclosure documents (e.g., registration statements, prospectus, preliminary prospectus).

8. The incorporators agree to use their best efforts to secure ratification of this agreement by the corporation's Board of Directors, as soon as the incorporation process has been completed.

9. The promoter will use his best efforts to secure valid, written subscriptions, on forms approved by the incorporators, for the sale of up to ____ shares of common stock at $ _____ per share, and up to ____ shares of preferred stock at $ _____ per share.

10. Unless the promoter obtains valid subscriptions totalling at least $ _____ within ____ days of the first date on which sale of stock first becomes permissible, the agreement will expire on that date unless the

promoter and incorporators agree to an extension. Unless $ _____ worth of stock has been subscribed to by the close date (as extended), the amounts paid by subscribers will be returned to them. The corporation (or the incorporators, if the corporation has not been formed) will reimburse the promoter for his out-of-pocket expenses in connection with obtaining subscriptions, but will have no other or further obligations to the promoter.

11. If the corporation is not in fact incorporated in the state of _____ on or before _____, 19 ____, this agreement will expire, and the incorporators will reimburse the promoter for his out-of-pocket expenses. Further, if the failure to incorporate is due to the wrongdoing or negligence of the incorporators, they will pay liquidated damages to the promoter in the sum of $ _____. However, if the failure to incorporate is due to causes beyond the control of the incorporators, they will not be liable beyond reimbursement of out-of-pocket expenses.

12. If the corporation is incorporated as contemplated, and if the promoter secures valid subscriptions for at least $ _____ worth of stock on or before _____, 19 ____, the promoter will be compensated by receiving one share of the corporation's common/preferred stock for every ____ shares for which he has obtained subscriptions. The incorporators will issue this stock as soon as possible after the corporation's organization meeting; it will be the promoter's sole compensation.

13. The promoter agrees not to make any statement, representation, or promise inconsistent with the prospectuses or other disclosure documents.

BUY-SELL AGREEMENT: INSURANCE-FUNDED, ENTITY PURCHASE

1. In this agreement, the *corporation* is _____, Inc., a company incorporated in the state of _____, with a principal office located at _____.

2. The *shareholders* and their addresses and stock ownership are as follows:

Name	Address	# of Shares Owned	% of Total

3. This agreement is designed to provide continuity of management for the corporation while also setting an estate tax valuation for the shareholders' stock, and provide liquidity for their estates.

4. The corporation agrees to maintain the following insurance policies, which it owns, on the lives of its shareholders:

Name of Insured	Name of Insurer	Face Amount

The corporation will be the sole owner of the policies, will hold the incidents of ownership, and agrees to make all premium payments on time.

5. The insurer is not a party to this agreement.

6. The corporation will review the insurance coverage every _____ years and will increase the coverage as necessary to provide funds for the buy-out of the interest of any stockholder who dies while the agreement is in force.

7. If any shareholder is or becomes uninsurable, or is rated up at or beyond _____ %, the corporation will maintain a reserve so that the reserve, plus investment appreciation, will be sufficient to buy out the shareholder's interest when added to any insurance obtainable on the shareholder's life.

8. Each shareholder agrees to make a will; maintain a valid will at all times; and to appoint an executor or other personal representative.

9. Each shareholder agrees to inform his or her personal representative of the terms of this agreement as amended.

10. On the death of a shareholder, his or her estate will sell all of his or her shares in the corporation to the corporation; the corporation will use insurance and reserve funds to buy these shares.

11. The corporation agrees to use its best efforts to promote prompt settlement of its claims under the policy, and to pay policy proceeds, up to the purchase price of the shares, to the executor or other personal representative, as soon as possible.

12. The corporation is entitled to keep any excess of policy proceeds over the amount needed to buy out the estate's shares.

13. If the policy proceeds are insufficient to meet the corporation's buy-out obligation, the corporation will:

☐ pay the difference in cash, within _____ days of settlement of the insurance claim

☐ give the executor or personal representative its promissory note, calling for payment in _____ equal monthly installments, beginning in the month of the settlement, with interest at an APR of _____ %.

14. All the shareholders agree to abide by the transfer restrictions set out in the transfer restrictions agreement signed _____, 19 _____. The corporation and all shareholders agree that these restrictions will be stated on the face of the share certificates.

15. The buy-out price will equal:

☐ book value for the shareholder's stock, on the date of his or her death

☐ $_____ per share [plus an annual increase of $_____ per share/ plus an annual increase equal to the increase in the Consumer Price Index over that year]

☐ the amount determined by an independent professional appraiser, whose fee will be paid by the corporation/the shareholder's estate

☐ the price set by arbitration according to the rules of the American Arbitration Association, with the arbitrator's fee being assumed by the corporation/the shareholder's estate.

16. This agreement will terminate automatically if the corporation is dissolved or placed in receivership, if the corporation becomes insolvent, or if all the shareholders then living sign another buy-sell agreement superseding this agreement.

17. This agreement, which is to be construed under the laws of the state of _____, binds and benefits the corporation, the signing shareholders, their heirs, assigns, and transferees.

State Statute Chart

	General Corporation Statute	Statutory Close Corporations	Incorporators	Reservation of Name	Articles of Incorporation: Contents	Bylaws	Initial Fees, Taxes	Qualification of Foreign Corporations	Preemptive Rights
ALABAMA	10-2A-1	10-2A-301	1/10-2A-90	10-2A-26(1)	10-2A-91	10-2A-45	10-2A-281, 40-14-22	10-2A-232, 40-14-21	10-2A-44
ALASKA	10.05.003	—	1/10.05.252	10.05.024	10.05.255	10.05.135	10.05.708	10.05.597	10.05.129
ARIZONA	10-101	10-201	2/10-053	10-009	10-054	10-027	10-129	10-106	10-026
ARKANSAS	64-101	—	1/64-501	64-108	64-502	64-513	64-1001	64-1201	64-212
CALIFORNIA	Corp §100	Corp §158, 418, 421	1/Corp. § 200	Corp. §201(c)	Corp. § 202, 205	Corp. § 211	Gov. 12180	Corp. §2105	Corp. §204(a)(2), 406
COLORADO	7-1-101	—	1/7-2-101	7-3-107	7-2-102	7-5-109	7-10-104	7-9-101	7-4-102, -110
CONNECTICUT	33-282	—	1/33-289	33-287	33-290	33-306	33-304	33-396	33-343
DELAWARE	T8 §101	T8 §342	1/T8 §101	—	T8 §102	T8 §109	T8 §391	T8 §371(b)	T8 §102(b)(3)
D.C.	29-301	—	3/29-346	29-309	29-347	29-324	29-399.22	29-399	29-323
FLORIDA	607.001	—	1/607.161	607.027	607.164	607.081	607.361	607.304	607.077
GEORGIA	14-2-1	—	1/14-2-170	14-2-41	14-2-172	14-2-176	14-2-371	14-2-310	14-2-111
HAWAII	416-1	—	1/416-11	416-13	416-11	416-79	416-97	418-1	416-24
IDAHO	30-1-2	—	1/30-1-53	30-1-10	30-1-54	30-1-27	30-1-128	30-1-106	30-1-26
ILLINOIS	Ch. 32 Art. 1-17	Ch. 32 ¶1201	1/Ch. 32 ¶2.05	Ch. 32 ¶4.10	Ch. 32 ¶2.10	Ch. 32 ¶2.25	Ch. 32 ¶15.10	Ch. 32 ¶13.05	Ch. 32 ¶6.50
INDIANA	23-1-2-1	—	1/23-1-3-1	23-1-2-4	23-1-3-2	23-1-2-8	23-3-2-2	23-1-11-1	23-1-2-6(i)
IOWA	496A.1	—	1/496A.48	496A.8	496A.49	496A.26	496A.124, .125	496A.103	496A.25
KANSAS	17-6001	17-7201	1/17-6001	17-7402	17-6002	17-6009	17-7502, -7506	17-7301	17-6002(b)
KENTUCKY	271A.005	—	1/271A.265	271A.045	271A.270	271A.135	271A.630	271A.520	271A.130
LOUISIANA	12:1	—	1/12:21	12:23(G)	12:24	12:28	12:171	12:301	12:72
MAINE	T13A §101	T13A §102(5)	1/T13A §402	T13A §302	T13A §403	T13A §601	T13A §1401	T13A §1201	T13A §623
MARYLAND	Corp. & Assn's. 2-101	Corp. & Assn's. 4-101	1/Corp. & Ass'n. 2-102	Corp. & Ass'n. 2-107	Corp. & Ass'n. 2-104	Corp. & Ass'n. 2-109	Corp. & Ass'n. 1-203, -204	Corp. & Ass'n. 7-101	Corp. & Ass'n. 2-205
MASSACHUSETTS	Ch. 156B §1	—	1/Ch. 156B §12	Ch. 156B §11(d)	Ch 156B §13	Ch. 156B §§12, 16, 17	Ch. 156B §114	Ch. 181 §1	Ch. 156B §20
MICHIGAN	450.1101	450.1463	1/450.1201	450.1215	450.1202	450.1231	450.2062	450.2011	450.1481
MINNESOTA	302A.001	302A.011, .457	1/302A.105	302A.117	302A.111	302A.181	302A.011 (11)	303.03	302A.413
MISSISSIPPI	79-3-1	—	2/79-3-103	79-3-15	79-3-105	79-3-51	79-3-255	79-3-211	79-3-49
MISSOURI	351.010	—	1/351.050	351.115	351.055	351.290	351.065, .658	351.570	351.305

114

	Cumulative Voting	Transfer Restrictions	Voting Trusts, Agreements	Franchise Tax	Corporate Income Tax	Annual Report	Professional Corporations Statute	General Partnership Statute	Limited Partnership Statute
ALABAMA	10-2A-53(d)	10-2A-41	10-2A-55	40-14-40	—	10-2A-260	10-4-383	10-8-1	10-9A-1
ALASKA	10.05.162	—	10.05.171	10.05.717	—	10.05.699	10.45.010	32.05.010	32.10.010
ARIZONA	10-033(D)	—	10-034	—	43-1111	10-125	10-901	29-201	29-301
ARKANSAS	64-219(D)	64-211	64-221	84-1801	—	84-1836	64-2001	65-101	65-501
CALIFORNIA	Corp. §708	Corp. §204(b)	Corp. §186, 706	Rev. & Tax §23151	Rev. & Tax §24591	Corp. 1502	Corp. §13400	Corp. §15001	Corp. §15501
COLORADO	7-4-116	—	7-4-117	—	39-22-301	7-10-101	12-36-134	7-60-101	7-62-101
CONNECTICUT	33-325	33-306a	33-338, -339	33-305	—	33-298	33-82	34-39	34-9
DELAWARE	T8 §214	T8 §202	T8 §218	T8 §503	—	T8 §374	T8 §601	T6 §1501	T6 §17-101
D.C.	29-327(d)	—	29-330	29-399.22	47-1807.2	29-398	29-601	41-101	41-201
FLORIDA	607.097(4)	—	607.104, .107	—	220.02	607.357	621.01	620.56	620.01
GEORGIA	14-2-117	—	14-2-121	48-13-71	48-7-21	14-2-350	14-7-1	14-8-1	14-9-20
HAWAII	416-74	—	416-75	—	235-71	416-95	416-141; Laws '85 HB346	425-1	425-22
IDAHO	30-1-33	30-1-23A	30-1-34	—	63-3025	30-1-126	30-1301	53-301	53-201
ILLINOIS	Ch. 32 ¶7.40	—	Ch. 32 ¶7.65, 7.70	Ch. 32 ¶15.35	Ch. 120 ¶2.201	Ch. 32 ¶14.05	Ch. 32 ¶415	Ch. 106½ ¶1	Ch. 106½ ¶44
INDIANA	23-1-2-9(k)	—	23-3-1-1	—	23-4-2-1	23-3-4-1	23-1.5-1-1	23-4-1-1	23-4-2-1
IOWA	496A.32	—	496A.33	496A.126	545.101	496A.121	496C.1	544.1	545.101
KANSAS	17-6504	17-6426	17-6508	17-7503	56-1a101	17-7514	17-2706	56-301	56-1a101
KENTUCKY	271A.175	—	271A.170	136.070	362.410	271A.615	274.005	362.150	362.410
LOUISIANA	12:75B	12:57(F)	12:78	47:601	CIV. Art. 2836	12:102	12:801-1171	9:3401	CIV. Art. 2836
MAINE	T13A §622	T13A §616	T13A §617, 619	—	T31 §151	T13A §1301	T13A §701	T31 §281	T31 §151
MARYLAND	Corp. & Ass'n. 2-104(b)(7)	Corp. & Ass'n. 2-211(d), 4-503	Corp. & Ass'n. 2-510	—	T81 §6	81 §251	Corp. & Ass'n. 5-101	Corp. & Ass'n. 9-101	Corp. & Ass'n. 10-101
MASSACHUSETTS	—	Ch. 156B §27	Ch. 156B §41A	Ch. 63 §54	Ch. 63C §1	Ch. 156B §109	Ch. 156A §1	Ch. 108A §1	Ch. 109 §1
MICHIGAN	450.1451	450.1472	450.1468, .1466	450.303	206.6	450.1911	450.221	449.1	449.1101
MINNESOTA	302A.215	302A.429	302A.453, .455	—	290.01	302A.821	319A.01	323.01	322A.01
MISSISSIPPI	79-3-63	—	79-3-65	27-13-1	27-7-29	79-3-249	79-9-1	79-12-1	79-13-1
MISSOURI	351.245	—	351.246	147.010	143.071, .431	351.120	356.010	358.010	359.010

State Statute Chart

	General Corporation Statute	Statutory Close Corporations	Incorporators	Reservation of Name	Articles of Incorporation: Contents	Bylaws	Initial Fees, Taxes	Qualification of Foreign Corporations	Preemptive Rights
MONTANA	35-1-101	35-1-515	1/35-1-201	35-1-302	35-1-202	35-1-214	35-1-1204	35-1-1001	35-1-511
NEBRASKA	21-2001	—	1/21-2051	21-2008	21-2052	21-2106	33-101	21-20, 105	21-2025
NEVADA	78.010	—	1/78.030	74.040	78.035	78.120	78.760	80.005; Laws '85 ch. 589	78.265
NEW HAMPSHIRE	293-A:1	—	1/293A:53	293A:9	293A:54	293A:27	293A:134, :136	293A:107	293A:26
NEW JERSEY	14A:1-1	15A:5-21	1/14A:2-6	14A:2-3	14A:2-7	14A:2-9	14A:15-1	14A:13-3	14A:5-29
NEW MEXICO	53-11-1	—	1/53-12-1	53-11-8	53-12-2	53-11-27	—	53-17-1	53-11-26
NEW YORK	BCL §101	BCL §620	1/BCL §401	BCL §303	BCL §402	BCL §601(a)	BCL §104-A; Tax §180	BCL §1301	BCL §622
NORTH CAROLINA	55-1	55-3.1	1/55-6	55-12(d)	55-7	55-16	55-155	55-131	55-56
NORTH DAKOTA	10-19-01	—	3/10-19-52	10-19-08	10-19-53	10-19-25	10-23-04	10-22-01	10-19-24
OHIO	1701.01	1701.59.1	1/1701.04 (A)	1701.05	1701.04	1701.11, 1701.59	111.16	1703.03	1701.15
OKLAHOMA	T18 §1.1	—	3/T18 §1.10	T18 §1.13	T18 §1.208	T18 §1.52	T18 §1.247	T18 §1.199	T18 §1.45
OREGON	57.002	—	1/57.306	57.050	57.311	57.141	57.761, .767	57.655	57.137
PENNSYLVANIA	T15 §1001	T15 §1371	1/T15 §1201	T15 §1203	T15 §1204	T15 §1304	—	T15 §2001	T15 §1611
RHODE ISLAND	7-1.1-1	7-1.1-51	1/7-1.1-47	7-1.1-8	7-1.1-48	7-1.1-31	7-1.1-121, -123	7-1.1-99	7-1.1-24
SOUTH CAROLINA	33-1-10	33-11-220	1/33-7-20	33-5-20	33-7-30	33-11-10	33-29-10	33-23-10	33-11-210
SOUTH DAKOTA	47-2-1	—	1/47-2-4	47-2-40	47-2-5	47-2-49	47-9-7(1)	47-8-1	47-3-47
TENNESSEE	48-1-101	—	1/48-1-201	48-1-209	48-1-202	48-1-812	48-1-1309	48-1-1101	48-1-713
TEXAS	Bus. Corp. Art. 1.01	Bus. Corp. Art. 12.01	1/Bus. Corp. Art. 3.01	Bus. Corp. Art. 2.06	Bus. Corp. Art. 3.02	Bus. Corp. Art. 2.23	Bus. Corp. Art. 10.01	Bus. Corp. Art. 8.01	Bus. Corp. Art. 2.22-1
UTAH	16-10-1	—	3/16-10-48	16-10-8	16-10-49	16-10-25	16-10-126	16-10-102	16-10-24
VERMONT	T18 §1801	—	1/T11 §1925	T11 §1856	T11 §1926	T11 §1873	T11 §2201	T11 §2101	T11 §1872
VIRGINIA	13.1-601	—	1/13.1-618	13.1-631	13.1-619	13.1-624	13.1-616; 58.1-2801	13.1-757	13.1-651
WASHINGTON	23A.04.010	—	1/23A.12.010	23A.08.060	23A.12.020	23A.08.230	23A.40.020	23A.32.010	23A.08.220
WEST VIRGINIA	31-1-1	—	1/31-1-26	31-1-12	31-1-27	31-1-17	11.12.79	31-1-49	31-1-90
WISCONSIN	180.01	180.995(1)	1/180.44	180.08	180.45	180.22	180.87	180.813	180.21
WYOMING	17-1-101	—	1/17-1-201	17-1-108	17-1-202	17-1-124	17-1-901	17-1-701	17-1-123

	Cumulative Voting	Transfer Restrictions	Voting Trusts, Agreements	Franchise Tax	Corporate Income Tax	Annual Report	Professional Corporations Statute	General Partnership Statute	Limited Partnership Statute
MONTANA	35-1-506(4)	35-1-203(b) 35-1-617	31-1-508	—	15-31-405	35-1-1101	35-4-108	35-10-101	35-12-501
NEBRASKA	21-2033	—	21-2034	21-303	77-2734	21-301	21-2201	67-101, -301	67-201
NEVADA	78.360	78.242	78.365	—	—	78.150	89.010	87.010	88.010
NEW HAMPSHIRE	293A:33	—	293A:34	293A:138	—	293A:132	294A:1	304A:1	305:1
NEW JERSEY	14A:5-24	14A:7-12	14A:5-21	54:10A-2	54:10E-1	14A:4-5	14A:17-1	42:1-1	42:2A-1
NEW MEXICO	53-11-33	—	53-11-34	53-3-13	7-2-3	53-5-2	53-6-1	54-1-1	54-2-1
NEW YORK	BCL §618	—	BCL §620, 621	Tax §209	—	Tax 211	BCL §1501	Partnership §1	Partnership §90
NORTH CAROLINA	55-67	—	55-72, -73	105-114	105-130	105-122	55B-1	59-31	59-1
NORTH DAKOTA	10-19-33	—	10-19-35	—	57-38-11	10-23-01	10-31-01	45-05-01	45-10.1-01
OHIO	1701.55	1701.25(B)	1701.49	5733.01	—	5733.02	1785.01	1775.01	1782.01
OKLAHOMA	T18 §1.68	—	T18 §1.66	T68 §1201	T68 §2353	T66 §21	T18 §801	T54 §201	T54 §174
OREGON	57-170(4)	—	57.175	57.767	314.011	57.755	58.005	68.010	69.150
PENNSYLVANIA	T15 §1505	T15 §1613.1	T15 §1511	T72 §7601	T72 §7401	—	T15 §2901	T59 §301	T59 §501
RHODE ISLAND	7-1.1-31(d)	7-1.1-21.1	7-1.1-32	44-12-1	44-11-1	7-1.1-118	7-5.1-1	7-12-1	7-13-1 & PL '85 Ch. 390 §2
SOUTH CAROLINA	33-11-200	—	33-11-160, 150	12-19-50	12-7-20	33-25-10	33-51-10	33-41-10	33-42-10
SOUTH DAKOTA	47-4-17; 47-5-6	—	47-4-23	—	—	47-9-1	47-11-1	48-1-1	48-6-1
TENNESSEE	48-1-712	—	48-1-714, -715	67-4-901	67-4-804	48-1-1308	48-3-401	61-1-101	61-2-101
TEXAS	Bus. Corp. Art. 2.29(D)	Bus. Corp. Art. 2-22	Bus. Corp. Art. 2.30	Tax 171.001	—	Tax 171.201	Civ. Art. 1528e §1	Civ. Art. 6132b §1	Civ. Art. 6132a §1
UTAH	16-10-31	—	16-10-32	—	59-17-1	16-10-121	16-11-1	48-1-1	48-2-1
VERMONT	T11 §1879(d)	—	T11 §1880	—	T32 §8101; Laws '84 Ch. 144	T11 §2151	T11 §801	T11 §1121	T11 §1391
VIRGINIA	13.1-669	13.1-649	13.1-670, -671	—	58.1-401	13.1-775	13.1-542	50-1	50-44 (to 1/1/87) 50-73.1 (Post-1/1/87)
WASHINGTON	23A.08.300	—	23A.08.330	23A.40.060	—	23A.40.032	18.100.010	25.04.010	25.10.010
WEST VIRGINIA	31-1-93	—	31-1-94	11-12-82	11-24-1	31-1-56a	—	47-8A-1	47-9-1
WISCONSIN	180.995 (10)	—	180.27	71.01(2)	71.07(2)	180.791	180.99	178.01	179.01
WYOMING	17-1-130	17-1-132	17-1-131	17-2-101	—	17-2-101	17-3-101	17-13-101	17-14-101

117

Table of Cases

Client Interviewing and Recordkeeping

First Bank & Trust Co. v. Zagoria, 250 Ga. 844, 302 SE2d 674 (1983)

South High Development Ltd. v. Weiver, Lippe & Gormley Co., CPA, 4 Oh.St.3d 1, 445 NE2d 1106 (1983)

U.S. v. Van Dyke, 696 F2d 957 (Fed.Cir. 1982)

Choosing the Business Form

Armco Inc. v. Hardesty, 467 U.S. 638 (1984)

Bank Building & Equipment Corp. of America v. Dir. of Revenue, CCH Corp.Law Guide ¶11,855 (Mo.Sup. 1985)

Eli Lilly & Co. v. Save-On Drugs Inc. 366 U.S. 276 (1961)

Kapp v. Naturelle, 611 F2d 703 (8th Cir. 1979)

Lavoie v. General Aerospace Materials Co. Inc., CCH Corp.Law Guide ¶11,914 (Mass. 1984)

Lord & Burnham Corp. v. Four Seasons Solar Prods. Corp., CCH Corp.Law Guide ¶11,839 (Del.Chancery 1984)

Maddux & Sons Inc. v. Local 395 Health & Welfare Trust Fund, 125 Ariz. 475, 610 P2d 477 (1980)

Mobil Oil Corp. v. Comm'r of Taxes of Vermont, 445 U.S. 425 (1980)

National Can Corp. v. Wash. State Dept. of Revenue, 105 Wash.2d 327, 715 P.2d 128 (1986), review granted 55 LW 3202

Oliver Promotions v. Tams-Witmark Music Library, 535 F.Supp. 1244 (SDNY 1982)

Pacamor Bearings, Inc. v. Molon Motors & Coil Inc., CCH Corp.Law Guide ¶11,856 (NY Sup. 1984)

Rees v. Mosaic Technologies, Inc., 53 LW 2135 (3d Cir. 1984)

Splaine v. Modern Electroplating Inc., CCH Corp.Law Guide ¶11,994 (Mass.App. 1984)

Trans-America Airlines, Inc. v. Kenton, CCH Corp.Law Guide ¶11,809 (Del.Sup. 1985)

Tyler Pipe Industries, Inc. v. Wash. State Dept. of Revenue, 105 Wash.2d 318, 715 P.2d 123 (1986), review granted 55 LW3202

Raising Start-Up Funds

Adventures in Wine, CCH Sec.Law Reporter ¶80,952 (1976-77 Transfer Binder)

Mary S. Krech Trust v. Lake Apartments, 642 F2d 98 (5th Cir. 1981)

Poe v. First National Bank, 597 F2d 895 (5th Cir. 1979)

SEC v. McDonald Investment Co., 343 FSupp 343 (D.Minn. 1972)

Tax Questions About the New Enterprise

Practical Tasks in Representing the Start-Up Business

The Corporate Balance of Power

Bibliography

Books

Cavich, Zolman, 3, 3A *Business Organizations with Tax Planning*. New York, New York: Matthew Bender, 1985.

Haynsworth, Harry J., *The Professional Skills of the Small Business Lawyer*. Philadelphia, Pennsylvania: ALI/ABA, 1984.

Haynsworth, Harry J., *Selecting the Form of a Small Business Entity*. Philadelphia, Pennsylvania: ALI/ABA, 1985.

Painter, William H., *Corporate and Tax Aspects of Closely Held Corporations*. Boston, Massachusetts: Little, Brown, 1981.

Rohrlich, Chester. *Organizing Corporate and Other Business Enterprises* (5th ed.). New York, New York: Matthew Bender, 1985.

Articles and Annotations

Boles, "Taxation: Tax Savings Available to the Family Held Close Corporation," 31 U. Kansas L. Rev. 649 (1983).

Brickey, "Corporate Criminal Liability: A Primer for Corporate Counsel," 40 Business Lawyer 129 (1984).

Bryan, "An Examination of the One Class of Stock Rule After the Subchapter S Revision Act of 1982," 3 Cooley L. Rev. 277 (1985).

Comment, "Closely Held Corporations," 37 Tax Lawyer 813 (1984).

Comment, "Corporate Compliance: Sample Procedures, Statements and Forms," 3 Preventive Law Reporter 87 (1984).

Comment, "Putting the House in Order: An Analysis of and Planning Considerations for the Home-Office Deduction," 14 U. Baltimore L. Rev. 522 (1985).

Comment, "Closely Held Corporations," 38 Tax Lawyer 847 (1985).

Dickey, "Buy-Sell Agreements can Conclusively Limit Value without Recapitalization Problems," 11 Estate Planning 268 (1984).

Kess, "Tax Tips—Putting One's Family on the Payroll," New York L. J. March 26, 1984, p. 1.

Kess, "New Rules for Records on Business Cars," New York L. J. December 9, 1985, p. 1.

Kessler & Richmond, "Has Congress Made the C Corporation Obsolete for the Small Business?" 7 Corp. L. Rev. 293 (1984).

Mann, "A Critical Analysis of the Statutory Close Corporation Supplement to the Model Business Corporation Act," 22 Am. Bus. L. J. 289 (1984).

Mendelson, "Planning for the Closely Held Corporation: Accounting Methods and Other Options," 43 Inst. on Federal Tax 7(21) (1985).

Miller, "Preserving the Privilege," 10 Litigation 20 (1984).

O'Neal, "Preventing Law: Tailoring the Corporate Form of Business to Ensure Fair Treatment of All," 49 Miss. L. J. 529 (1978)

Peeples, "The Use and Misuse of the Business Judgment Rule in the Close Corporation," 60 Notre Dame L. Rev. 456 (1985).

Rea, "A Written Program for Preventive Law Activity," 2 Preventive Law Rep. 177 (1984).

Sands, "Key Concepts in the Taxation of Close Corporations and their Shareholders," 89 Commercial L. J. 560 (1984).

Schack, "Right to Privacy for Business Entities," 24 Santa Clara L. Rev. 53 (1984).

Starr, "The S Corporation: Is it the Right Choice?" 43 Inst. on Federal Tax 5(40) (1985).

Thomas, "Solving the Riddle of Rev. Proc. 83-25," 15 Tax Adviser 677 (1984).

Warren, "A Review of Regulation D," 33 Am. U. L. Rev. 355 (1984).

Weissman, "Unitary Taxation: Its History and Recent Supreme Court Treatment," 48 Albany L. Rev. 48 (1983).

Willins, "Incorporating a Partnership: The Application of Rev. Rul. 70-239," 15 Tax Adviser 353 (1984).

Wolfe & DeJong, "The S Corporation as an Alternative Form of Business Organization," 32 DePaul L. Rev. 811 (1983).

Wootton, "Advising Small Businesses on the Election of Subchapter S Status," 30 Prac. Lawyer 13 (1984).

Yelen, "Choosing the S Corporation as the Preferred Entity," 42 Inst. on Federal Tax 13-1(33) (1984).

Index